The Carpenter

The Carpenter

A Story About the Greatest Success Principles of All

JON GORDON

WILEY

Cover image: © iStockphoto/sorendis (background); © iStockphoto/blackwaterimages (toolbox)
Cover design: Michael J. Freeland

Copyright © 2014 by Jon Gordon. All rights reserved.

Published by John Wiley & Sons, Inc., Hoboken, New Jersey.
Published simultaneously in Canada.

Note: "Social Connect" is a fictitious company.

No part of this publication may be reproduced, stored in a retrieval system, or transmitted in any form or by any means, electronic, mechanical, photocopying, recording, scanning, or otherwise, except as permitted under Section 107 or 108 of the 1976 United States Copyright Act, without either the prior written permission of the Publisher, or authorization through payment of the appropriate per-copy fee to the Copyright Clearance Center, 222 Rosewood Drive, Danvers, MA 01923, (978) 750-8400, fax (978) 646-8600, or on the web at www.copyright.com. Requests to the Publisher for permission should be addressed to the Permissions Department, John Wiley & Sons, Inc., 111 River Street, Hoboken, NJ 07030, (201) 748-6011, fax (201) 748-6008, or online at www.wiley.com/go/permissions.

Limit of Liability/Disclaimer of Warranty: While the publisher and author have used their best efforts in preparing this book, they make no representations or warranties with respect to the accuracy or completeness of the contents of this book and specifically disclaim any implied warranties of merchantability or fitness for a particular purpose. No warranty may be created or extended by sales representatives or written sales materials. The advice and strategies contained herein may not be suitable for your situation. You should consult with a professional where appropriate. Neither the publisher nor the author shall be liable for damages arising herefrom.

For general information about our other products and services, please contact our Customer Care Department within the United States at (800) 762-2974, outside the United States at (317) 572-3993 or fax (317) 572-4002.

Wiley publishes in a variety of print and electronic formats and by print-on-demand. Some material included with standard print versions of this book may not be included in e-books or in print-on-demand. If this book refers to media such as a CD or DVD that is not included in the version you purchased, you may download this material at http://booksupport.wiley.com. For more information about Wiley products, visit www.wiley.com.

ISBN 978-0-470-88854-4 (cloth); ISBN 978-1-118-91525-7 (ebk);
ISBN 978-1-118-91526-4 (ebk)

Printed in the United States of America.
SKY10031381_111121

For Kathryn, who stood right beside me as we built a life, a family, and a mission together.

Contents

	Foreword by Ken Blanchard	ix
	Acknowledgments	xi
1	Collapse	1
2	Rest	5
3	The Carpenter	9
4	Stressed	15
5	Busy	17
6	Design Your Masterpiece	19
7	Be a Craftsman	25
8	You Will Know	29
9	Everybody Loves the Carpenter	33
10	Believe	37
11	Talk to Yourself instead of Listening to Yourself	41
12	Sarah	45
13	Chaos	49
14	The Greatest Success Strategy of All	53
15	Love Is a Commitment	59

16	People > Furniture	63
17	The Second Greatest Success Strategy of All	67
18	The Sandwich	75
19	The Third Greatest Success Strategy of All	77
20	Love, Serve, Care	83
21	Value	85
22	The Heart of Success	87
23	Failing	91
24	Success Takes Time	93
25	The Gift of Failure	95
26	Unfinished Work	99
27	Courage	101
28	A Glimmer of Hope	105
29	Be the Mission	109
30	All for One	113
31	Progress	117
32	Everything Is Spiritual	121
33	Creating the Impossible	125
34	Build	129
35	Success Is Meant to Be Shared	131
	Tools for Success	*135*
	Bring the Greatest Success Principles to Your Team and Organization	*137*
	Other Books by Jon Gordon	*139*

Foreword

In my sessions with managers around the world, I often begin by asking, "How many of you think you are leaders? Please raise your hands if you do." I'm always amazed that less than 20 percent raise their hands. Why is it that these managers—whose jobs are defined by leading others—do not think they are leaders?

The answer is that most people, managers included, believe leadership is defined by the title and position they hold. The managers who don't raise their hands believe they don't have titles that are fancy enough or positions that are high enough to call themselves leaders.

These managers probably didn't have a father like mine. A highly decorated admiral of the Navy, my dad taught me priceless lessons about leadership. I'll never forget when I was elected president of my seventh-grade class. When I came home from school all pumped up and proud, Dad said, "Congratulations, Ken. But now that you are president, don't ever use your position. Great leaders are great because people trust and respect them, not because they have power."

That's the message of Jon Gordon's wonderful new book, *The Carpenter*. I encourage you to think of the main character as a mentor. He will teach you that any human being who loves, serves, and cares is a leader.

If you're a businessperson, shift your focus from "winning"—whatever that means to you—to using your business to love, serve, and build up others. If you do this, you will succeed and your business will grow in ways you never imagined.

You'll also learn that to achieve genuine success, you must help others. Your first job in life is not to judge and evaluate people, but to help them succeed in whatever they're doing. In other words, success is meant to be shared.

I am excited that you have decided to read this book. *The Carpenter* can change your life for the better. And you, in turn, can change the lives of the people around you—who in turn can change the lives of those they touch. And just maybe, one person at a time, we can change the world.

—KEN BLANCHARD,
coauthor of *The One Minute Manager*®
and *Leading at a Higher Level*

Acknowledgments

I want to acknowledge Walter Isaacson, the author of *Steve Jobs*, who inspired the story the carpenter tells about his father being unwilling to use cheap wood for the back of the cabinet. Steve Jobs' father taught him the same lesson while building a fence and I was inspired to adapt this story to my own book.

Thank you to Erwin McManus, whose talk on being a little crazy in order to be a success inspired what I wrote on this topic.

Thank you to Joey Green, author of *The Road to Success Is Paved with Failure*, for the examples of famous failures that I shared in this book.

Thank you to Frank Gambuzza for telling me his secret to why his hair salon is so successful.

Thank you to my publisher, Matt Holt; my editor, Shannon Vargo; and the rest of the team at Wiley for believing in this book and sharing it with the world.

Thank you to my wife, Kathryn, for reading the manuscript and making great suggestions and changes as always.

Thank you to my friends Dan Britton and Joshua Medcalf for reading the book and sharing insights and suggestions to make it better.

Thank you to my team, including Daniel Decker, Brooke Trabert, and Anne Carlson, for all your support and for making it possible for me to do what I do best.

Thank you to all the craftsmen and craftswomen who approach life and work as artists.

Thank you to all those who love, serve, and care, and become the mission.

Most of all I thank God for the Carpenter who saved me in 2006 and transformed my life, heart, and soul forever.

Chapter 1
Collapse

The last thing Michael remembered before waking up in the hospital was running through the city streets and thinking about ways to build his company. Now he was lying on his back with wires and machines connected to his body as his wife, Sarah, sat by his side and a nurse stood over him.

"What am I doing here?" he asked groggily. "Did I get hit by a car or something?"

"You passed out on your run," answered Sarah, who was crying and shaking. In all the years she had known him, she couldn't recall him having more than a cold, never mind being in the hospital.

"How? Why?" he asked.

"That's what the doctor is trying to figure out right now. He's reviewing your tests and should be in shortly," the nurse said.

"I hope I'm okay," Michael said as he looked around the room and then at Sarah. She tried to smile and act reassuring but she couldn't. She was scared and expecting bad news.

Michael lifted his arm and felt a bandage and lump on his head. "How did I get here?"

"The ambulance brought you. Your head hit the ground pretty hard. The EMTs told us that a man saw you collapse and helped you. He used his shirt to stop the bleeding and called 911. He just might have saved your life."

"Who was it?"

"They didn't get his name. He just gave them that card sitting on your table."

Sarah picked up the card and showed it to Michael. It was a simple plain white card with only the word *Carpenter* and a phone number in black, bold ink.

"Not much of a marketer," Michael said, coming to his senses and regaining his sense of humor.

Sarah's nervousness turned to laughter as she shook her head. Even while in the hospital he was thinking about business. She was thankful, at least, that he was feeling more normal.

In that moment the doctor walked in and stood over Michael's bed. "Well, the good news is that you didn't have a heart attack like I had feared," he said as he shook Michael's hand.

"Heart attack!" Michael exclaimed. "I'm too young to have a heart attack!"

"Not necessarily," the doctor countered. "In fact, your body is warning you that you better slow down and manage your stress or you'll experience the real thing before too long. Have you been under a lot of stress lately?"

Michael and Sarah looked at each other. "We own a business," Sarah said. "We've been building it together, and with two kids, it's been a whirlwind."

"Well I advise you to slow down," the doctor said as he made eye contact with Michael. "No business or success is worth your health and life. I want you to rest for a few weeks before heading back to work. It will do your heart and your head some good. You have a minor concussion as well. Nothing major or serious but we want your head to heal, too."

Michael looked at Sarah. Rest was the last thing he needed with everything they had going on.

The doctor walked toward the door but before leaving the room he turned around and said, "You're lucky this was just a warning. I see people all the time who don't get a warning like this. Remember, life gives us warnings for a reason. Learn from this. Do things differently. Your health, kids, and future grandkids will be thankful you did."

Chapter 2

Rest

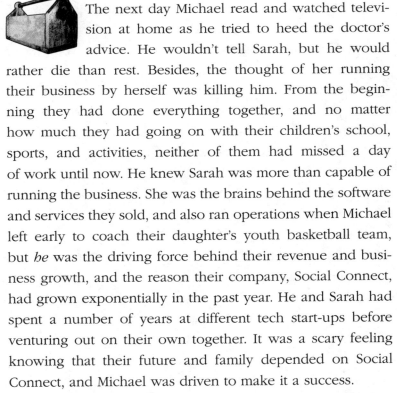

The next day Michael read and watched television at home as he tried to heed the doctor's advice. He wouldn't tell Sarah, but he would rather die than rest. Besides, the thought of her running their business by herself was killing him. From the beginning they had done everything together, and no matter how much they had going on with their children's school, sports, and activities, neither of them had missed a day of work until now. He knew Sarah was more than capable of running the business. She was the brains behind the software and services they sold, and also ran operations when Michael left early to coach their daughter's youth basketball team, but *he* was the driving force behind their revenue and business growth, and the reason their company, Social Connect, had grown exponentially in the past year. He and Sarah had spent a number of years at different tech start-ups before venturing out on their own together. It was a scary feeling knowing that their future and family depended on Social Connect, and Michael was driven to make it a success.

But now his strongest character traits—drive, work ethic, and passion—were affecting his health, and he had no idea what to do. He felt like a baseball pitcher being told he could no longer use his fastball. He wanted to go back to work immediately, but Sarah wouldn't allow it. "You'll be divorced before that happens," she told him. "A few weeks won't make or break our business, but it will make or break your health."

Unable to change Sarah's mind, Michael spent his time pacing around the house trying to relax, and failing miserably at it. He stopped in front of his flat-screen TV in the family room, sat on the couch, and thought of the entertainment center Sarah wanted to build. For the first time he could picture it. At first he thought of building it himself, but then laughed at the idea. His father had always told him that he better make a lot of money because he would need to hire people to fix things around the house. And Michael did something even better: He married a handy woman who could fix things. Her dad was a mechanic, her brothers were plumbers, and when something broke in the house, the kids went to her instead of him. Yet, building entertainment centers was beyond even her skill set.

Michael then thought of the carpenter who had saved him and remembered he had his card. *I really should call to thank him*, he thought. But what do you say to a stranger who saved your life? "Hi. You saved my life. Can you build entertainment centers?" Michael found the card on the counter and decided he was just going to say thank you and ask him where he could send a gift. He called the number and after a few rings Michael heard the voice of the man who saved his life: "Hi, I'm not answering my phone right now because I'm building kitchen cabinets at 111 Main Street. I'm putting my heart and soul into these cabinets so I won't be returning calls until I'm finished with the job. Please know

I will give the same attention and care to your work, as well. If you need to talk to me feel free to come by 111 Main Street during my lunch break at noon."

Michael shook his head. A carpenter who doesn't say his name on his voicemail and won't return calls to potential clients. *How does he have any clients?* Michael wondered. Not only does this guy need a new business card, he also needs a lot of help to build his business.

Chapter 3

The Carpenter

A few days later, after helping Sarah and the kids get ready for school in the morning, Michael took a slow walk in the park. It wasn't something he wanted to do. It was something Sarah made him do. The doctor advised him to do some light exercise to keep his blood flowing and also said he could do any of his normal activities, besides work, that didn't cause him stress. After walking, Michael grabbed a water bottle in the kitchen and saw the carpenter's card still sitting on the counter. He looked at it for a few moments and decided it was time to say thank you in person.

It's not every day you get to meet the person who saved your life, Michael thought, as he sat in bumper-to-bumper city traffic. *What if I don't like him? We know he's a horrible marketer. What if he turns out to be a horrible person?* Michael considered a number of possibilities as he passed the road construction that was causing the traffic, and decided the man deserved a thank you regardless of the kind of person he was. After all, it's not every day you need someone to save your life.

At noon Michael pulled up to 111 Main Street, a large, beautiful, newly constructed home with a circular driveway packed with pick-up trucks. When he walked in the front door he saw a bunch of men painting the walls and ceiling as the sounds of hammering and sawing filled the air. He walked to the kitchen and noticed a dark-skinned man with shoulder-length brown hair. He was dressed in blue jeans, brown sandals, and a white t-shirt, and sat at the kitchen table eating lunch. When the man looked up and saw Michael, his eyes lit up. He ran toward him with a big smile and wrapped his arms around him. "Michael, it's great to see you. You sure look a lot better than the last time I saw you," he said before letting out a hearty laugh. "I've been wondering how you were doing. What a nice surprise!"

"I'm doing well," Michael said awkwardly. He was not a big hugger and didn't expect such a warm welcome from a stranger.

The carpenter stepped back and stared at Michael's forehead before placing his finger near the cut. "It's healing well," he said with a big, radiant smile. "I'm thankful to see that."

"Yeah, me too," Michael said nervously. "I want to thank you for helping me that day."

"Oh it was nothing. You would have done the same for me," said the carpenter as he walked back to the kitchen table and motioned for Michael to sit down with him.

"What exactly happened?" asked Michael.

"Well, it was really early and the sun was just coming up. I was walking to this job, which is how I get to all my jobs, and the next thing I know, I see you running, and then—*bam!*—you go down like someone shot you. Your head hit the ground hard and started bleeding pretty heavily. I took my shirt off and compressed it against your forehead to stop the bleeding and called for help. You were out of it, but when I asked you your name you mumbled it clear enough for me to hear and tell the police when they showed up. I figured you had people who would be concerned about you when you didn't come back from your run."

"Wow. I can't believe you did all that to help me. Thank you so much. They told me at the hospital that you were a true hero. And you left your card for me," Michael said as he reached into his pocket and held it up.

"I did," said the carpenter.

"But it doesn't have your name on it. I don't even know your name."

"Oh, forgive me. I usually write my name on the card. It makes it more personal. But with them rushing you off to the hospital, I forgot. I apologize for not properly introducing myself. My name is J. Emmanuel," he said as he smiled and reached out to shake Michael's hand. "J. is actually my first name and Emmanuel is my middle name. But everyone just calls me J."

"Is J short for Jason or is it J-A-Y?" asked Michael.

"No, it's just a J and a period. My parents believed I was unique."

"Okay, J.," Michael said with a smile as he shook his hand. "It's nice to officially put a name—or an initial—to the man who saved my life."

The carpenter laughed as he got up from the table and walked over to the cabinets he was building. "I'm just glad I was there to help. You know, when I'm not walking around the city saving people's lives, I build things like this," he said with a smile, as he proudly showed off his woodwork.

Michael may not have been handy, but he knew quality work when he saw it and these were the most exquisite cabinets he had ever seen. The guy needed help with his marketing, but he certainly didn't need help with his carpentry. "They look incredible," Michael said. "Do you build entertainment centers, too?"

"I can build anything, and I have built just about everything," said the carpenter.

"That's great because it just so happens that my doctor and wife are making me take a few weeks off from work to relax and get better, and I need someone to help me build an entertainment center. I would love to repay you for saving my life," said Michael, figuring he could use the work.

"I'm honored that you would want me to build something special in your home, but please know you don't have to repay me for anything," said the carpenter as he put his hands on his heart. "I give and expect nothing in return. It's a beautiful way to live and work. If you want me to build your entertainment center, I would love to but please choose me because of my work, not because you feel obligated. Never do anything out of obligation. Do everything with gratitude and love. It's much more powerful that way."

Michael nodded as he thought about what the carpenter said. There was clearly more than meets the eye with this guy. He had never met anyone quite like him. Most people would just take the job, but not him. He wanted to be hired for doing quality work. J. was definitely a different breed and he seemed like a man of principle; besides, a little philosophy never hurt. Plus, he was very skilled. Michael would have hired him regardless of whether J. had saved his life. Being the great listener and salesman that Michael was, he stood up and said, "Okay, how does this sound, 'I am grateful that you saved my life, and because of your skill, I would *love* to have you build an entertainment center in my home'?"

"That sounds wonderful," the carpenter said, laughing as he walked over and patted Michael on the back. J. knew they weren't completely on the same page yet, but they would be soon. He could tell that Michael was a lifelong learner, and that meant they could build more than an entertainment center.

"When can you start?" asked Michael.

"I am almost finished with these cabinets and am booked for months, but I will make time for you and will rearrange some things. How about we start the day after tomorrow?"

"Sounds great. Here's my address," Michael said as he wrote the information on the back of one of his cards and handed it to J. "I appreciate you fitting me in. I didn't realize you are so busy."

"Oh, I am very busy. In fact they tell me I'm the busiest carpenter in the city."

"Really?" Michael said, sounding very surprised. "Why is that?"

"It's because of the principles that guide my business. I know the greatest success strategies of all," said the carpenter.

Michael was now very curious. Surely, he wasn't talking about his business card or marketing prowess. "What are they?" he asked.

"I will tell you when I see you in two days. I have a few other people who came to see me," the carpenter said, before giving Michael a hug good-bye and waving to the line of people waiting to talk to him. And as Michael walked out of the kitchen and passed the group of people waiting to hire J., he started to believe that the carpenter might be a lot smarter than he thought.

Chapter 4
Stressed

Michael woke up in the middle of the night and looked at the clock: 3:33 AM. He tried to go back to bed, but couldn't. He had another nightmare where he was fighting for his life against faceless people, battling for unknown reasons. In this nightmare he was screaming for help but no one could hear him. Everything was happening in slow motion as he tried to evade his attackers. They were closing in and were about to ambush him when he woke up in a deep sweat with his heart racing and head pounding. He had been having trouble sleeping the past few months, which had contributed to the stress that ultimately caused him to pass out during his run. While he was recuperating the last few days he had read a book on stress and sleep that described the vicious cycle he was caught in, in which stress affects your ability to sleep, and then a lack of sleep causes more stress.

Sarah and his friends kept telling him that he needed to relax, but how could he relax when he was building a business, and his family and company were depending on him? How could he relax when he had been in sales his whole life, and now an entire company was looking to him for leadership and guidance? Every decision he made mattered and had repercussions for employees, clients, and families. When he was in sales, all he had to do was sell and collect a large paycheck. Now he was the one signing the paychecks. He had mastered the art of sales over the years, but no one had taught him how to lead people, and nothing could have prepared him for the success and challenges Social Connect was experiencing. He wouldn't tell anyone, but he felt unprepared and inadequate, and feared letting his wife, family, and company down. This was everything he had worked his entire career for, and he couldn't fail. *How could anyone relax with this kind of burden?* Michael wondered, as he gave up on going back to sleep and walked down the hall to his home office. He turned on the computer to look at Social Connect's sales numbers from the last few days. Sarah had forbidden him from checking on sales, but he needed to know for his own well-being. If she caught him looking, he would tell the truth: Not looking at the numbers was causing him more stress than seeing them.

He was relieved to see that sales were steady and some new business was still coming in, despite his absence, but he worried the trend wouldn't continue the longer he was away from the business. *I have to get back to work*, he thought. *Not being there is killing me more than being there would.* He then left a voicemail for his assistant asking her to call him when she got to the office to give him an update. Then, he walked to the other side of the house to check on his kids, who were sound asleep in their rooms. The quiet before the storm, he thought.

Chapter 5

Busy

When Sarah and the kids walked into the kitchen that morning Michael already had breakfast waiting for them. He wanted to make them eggs, but of course they were out of them. They ran out of a lot of things since they didn't usually have much time to go shopping. Every day was a race against the clock to get the kids to school, get to work, get to meetings, get to after-school events, get dinner, get to bed, and get up and do it all again. Time to shop was a luxury.

"Daddy, will you be coaching basketball practice today?" his nine-year-old daughter asked, as they spent their usual 10 minutes of family time at the kitchen table. Michael looked at Sarah and then said, "I don't know. Ask Mommy."

"No, Daddy gets too intense and yells too much, which is not good for him right now," said Sarah.

"You don't think *this* is stressful?" Michael said, raising his voice as his seven-year-old son spilled his cereal bowl on the table. "If I can do this, I can coach. Same thing!"

"You only yell a little bit at home," his son said with such naivety that Sarah and Michael burst out in laughter.

"Daddy will be coaching in a few weeks, but for right now he won't be at practice," Sarah said as Michael sighed.

"Time to make the bus," Michael said as the family hopped up from the table and scattered to get their things. Of course, his son couldn't find his shoes for a few minutes, and when he found them the laces were tied so tight that he couldn't put them on. And, of course, they were double-knotted so Michael had to undo the knots before untying the shoes and helping his son put them on. As soon as they solved the shoe conundrum, they ran to the bus stop and barely caught the bus, only to hear their daughter yell out the window that she forgot her book report. So once again, Michael was going to be bringing one of her projects to school.

When he and Sarah walked in the front door he looked at her and said, "This is more stressful than work."

"Soon. Soon. You will be back," she said before kissing him good-bye, grabbing her bag, and racing out the door to her car, where she would be spending a lot of time sitting in bumper-to-bumper traffic on her way to an important meeting.

Michael walked into the family room and looked at the wall where the carpenter would be building an entertainment center tomorrow, and wondered if his success strategies included stress reduction because he needed to be able to get back to work so he could be a success.

Chapter 6

Design Your Masterpiece

The doorbell rang the next morning shortly after Sarah and the kids left for school. Michael opened the door and the carpenter was standing there with a big smile and dressed in the same blue jeans, sandals, and white t-shirt.

He gave Michael a big hug, something Michael figured he would have to get use to if he wanted his entertainment center built. "How are you feeling?" the carpenter asked.

"I'm feeling pretty good," answered Michael. "Thanks for asking. So where are your tools and stuff?"

"Oh, I don't need them. I won't be building anything today. Before you build a masterpiece you must design it. It's the same way with life, you know. Too many people go through life living by chance, but when you live by design and know the life you want to create, you are able to create a masterpiece instead of a piece of junk."

Michael couldn't help but think about what his life looked like. Was he living by chance or by design? Was he creating a masterpiece? Or, was he causing his body to burn out and fail?

"So tell me what you had in mind," said the carpenter as they walked into the house and toward the family room.

Michael picked up a home design magazine from the table and showed J. the page that Sarah had earmarked for him. "My wife absolutely loves the look of this. Can you build something like this?"

"Of course. I can build anything. Now that I see it, I can design it. Do you have a piece of paper and a pencil?"

Michael reached into the "everything drawer" filled with all the kids' pencils, markers, and erasers, pulled out a piece of paper and a pencil, and handed them to the carpenter, who immediately started drawing frantically. A few minutes later he lifted up the paper for Michael to see. "How does this look?"

"That's it! I can't believe you drew all that so quickly."

"It's a gift. I see it and I am able to create it."

"Sarah will love it!" Michael exclaimed.

"Excellent. Now that we know what you want your masterpiece to look like, we can begin the process of creating it. And now I must ask you, Michael, a very important question beyond furniture: What does your life's masterpiece look like?"

Michael didn't know what to say as he shook his head and pondered the question. He knew they were going to talk about more than entertainment centers, but he didn't know they were going to get personal about his life. "You know when you mentioned creating your masterpiece, I was thinking about whether I was creating a masterpiece or not. Truth is, I thought I knew what it looked like and I was on my way to building it with our company, but that was before I collapsed and went to the hospital. Now I'm realizing that without my health, I can't create my masterpiece. I guess my picture of what it looks like is a little blurry right now."

"That's okay. Blurry things can be brought into focus with the right questions and better strategies," the carpenter said as he lifted his arms into the air to stretch. "People often ask me, as you did the other day, why I am so busy and successful, and I believe it started with asking what success looked like when I started my career. I asked what it would look like while I was thriving in my life and career and what it would look like at the end of my life. I began with the end in mind and worked backward. I had a compelling vision for my life and worked toward making it come to fruition every day."

"I know this well. We did the same thing when we started our company, Social Connect," said Michael. "I read that every great leader and organization does the same thing. They see the world not as it is, but as it could be. Then, before they begin an initiative, project, product launch, season, or campaign, they ask themselves what the world will look like when they are finished. Once you have a vision of what could be, and know what the world looks like, you are ready to design, create, and launch. After reading about all the successful people and organizations that did this, we envisioned how we could change the world with Social Connect."

"I love it!" exclaimed the carpenter. "And now you must do the same thing with your life. Now you must ask yourself these questions: What does it look like when you are at your healthiest, strongest, and best? What does your family situation look like while you are pursuing success in your work? Are you ignoring the people you love the most or making more time for them? What matters most? What priorities drive you each day? What are you doing that makes you come alive? What are you doing to live and share your purpose?

When you look back on your life what do you want to be able to say about it? How do you want to feel? What will you have wanted to accomplish? What legacy will you have left? Years from now people will be telling stories about you, and you must ask yourself what kind of stories you want them to tell. Powerful questions like these help you design and create a great life."

"Did you ask these questions of your life?" Michael asked, wanting to know more about where the carpenter found such profound thoughts.

"I did. And they made all the difference. They helped me create an amazing life and a very successful career. My children are grown and now have children of their own. And while my design did not include the loss of my dear wife, most times the perfect design must give way to the ultimate Creator's master plans. But the times we had together were the greatest moments of my life, and designing my masterpiece and my other success strategies made them possible. So in the end, when I look back on my life, I will smile at what I have done rather than regret what I haven't."

"I'm so sorry about your loss," said Michael as he looked closely at the carpenter's face. The youthfulness of his face defied his years but his wisdom did not. "You are much more than a carpenter, aren't you?" he asked.

"I am indeed. Over the years I have built more than furniture and cabinets. I have helped people build their lives, careers, and teams. I didn't plan it this way. It just happened. It is my purpose and I receive it. After all, material things eventually fade away. No matter how beautiful an entertainment center we build, it won't last forever. It may not even last a lifetime. But the leaders and people I build up, the people I invest in, the relationships I develop, and the success strategies I share—that is what endures and ripples through eternity. While I'm excited to build this entertainment center with you, I'm even more excited to help you build your life."

Michael rubbed his face as the carpenter's words caused him to think of all the challenges that confronted him. "Will your leadership strategies help me be a better leader?" he asked.

"Of course! My strategies permeate every aspect of life. They help leaders lead, salespeople sell, coaches coach, parents parent, teachers teach. They are the ultimate success strategies that help people build whatever it is they want to build. Whether it's a family, a team, a business, a school, a career, or an organization, my tools for success are powerful, and three of my strategies are the greatest of them all.

"But you won't have to just take my word for it. You will be able to put these strategies into action. You can make them a habit and they will become a part of who you are and how you live and work. When you do, you will see how simple yet powerful and transforming they are. These strategies do not come from me but from my father and I have witnessed their power firsthand in my own life and the lives of others. Most people don't implement them because they don't believe it could be so simple. They think a strategy has to be big and complex to work but in reality the most successful strategies are extremely simple. Simple is powerful. Just remember that simple does not mean easy. You still have to take action."

The carpenter coughed and then cleared his throat, which was becoming a little hoarse. He continued. "Here's what I know, Michael. Our lives intersected that day for a reason. I wasn't meant to just save your life. I was meant to help you create it. When we build a better you, you will build a better business that endures the tests of time. So, are you ready to learn more of my favorite success strategies as you begin to design your masterpiece?"

"Yes, I am but I have to warn you, it's going to take a lot to turn this guy and this life into a masterpiece. I'm a little broken down as you know from my run the other day."

"That's okay. Some of my best work has been taking things that are broken and making them whole again. I'm up for the challenge. What do you say we go get the wood and materials we need for the entertainment center and I'll share more on the way?"

Chapter 7

Be a Craftsman

"Once you design your masterpiece, you must be a craftsman in your approach to your life and work," the carpenter said as they drove down the highway toward the store. "All success starts with being a craftsman."

"But your card says *carpenter* on it," Michael asked in an inquisitive tone. "Why not put *craftsman*?"

"Because everyone understands what a carpenter does. Having *craftsman* on the card would scare some people away. People feel comfortable with the term *carpenter* so I do it for marketing purposes," he said proudly as Michael smirked. He was excited to learn the carpenter's success strategies, but didn't believe marketing was one of them.

The carpenter continued, "I get jobs as a carpenter but I approach my work as a craftsman."

"What's the difference?" asked Michael.

"A carpenter builds things. A craftsman creates a work of art. While most people approach their work with the mindset that they just want to get it done, craftsmen are more concerned with who they are becoming and what they are creating rather than how fast they finish it. After all, it's no use finishing something if it's not a work of art.

"As a craftsman, I know the things I build won't last forever but I work and create as though they will. I pour my heart and soul into everything I build, knowing that all that I create is a reflection of me. When I create art, I feel energized, and I energize all those who experience my work. And with each creation I become more of the person I was meant to be."

Michael stopped at a red light and turned to the carpenter. "Hearing you say 'heart and soul' reminded me of what your voicemail greeting says. I was surprised that you didn't return phone calls because, you said, you were putting your heart and soul into your current project and that you would do the same for other people who called you."

The carpenter laughed. "Yes, that's something else I do for marketing purposes. It's not a gimmick. It's the truth, and I started saying that out of necessity really. I didn't have someone who could return calls for me, so I had to decide what was most important about my work and I realized it was the art I created. I knew the work I do as an artist must come first and I couldn't allow distractions to get in the way. So in my voicemail I told people the truth. I don't return calls because I'm focused on doing the work and putting my heart and soul into it. If I spent all the time necessary to call people back, I wouldn't have the energy to create great art. So people come see me during my lunch hour, we talk, and everything is lined up then. If I'm working at a place where people can't visit, then I tell them they can meet me at my favorite burrito shop after I'm finished. It's not a strategy I recommend for most people, but it works for me. The fact that I'm so busy tells me people are more interested in the work I do than how fast I return their calls.

"The world is filled with those who get things done the fastest and the cheapest, but it needs more artists, craftsmen, and craftswomen. When you become a craftsman in a world of carpenters, you will stand out and people will clamor to work with you."

Chapter 8

You Will Know

"When did you first realize the difference between a carpenter and a craftsman?" asked Michael.

The carpenter paused for a few moments as a tear ran down his cheek. "When I was a teenager, I was watching my father make a cabinet for the first time. He was using the finest and most expensive wood available. We didn't have a lot of money so I asked him why he didn't use cheaper wood for the back of the cabinet, which no one would see. My father shook his head and said no. I asked him why not, since no one will know. My father replied, 'I will know. You will know. We will know.'

"That's when I knew what it meant to be an artist. That's when I knew I would be a craftsman even though the costs were greater. The wood was more expensive; the work required more energy, focus, and effort; the process was filled with more sweat and failure; and the years and tears it took to master my craft were greater, but it was the only way. My father taught me that when I fall in love with the process, I will love what the process creates."

"It's not easy," Michael said, knowing the sweat, tears, and years he put into his career in sales before launching Social Connect.

"No, it's not easy at all," the carpenter continued, becoming more animated than Michael had ever seen him. "Everyone can be a craftsman or craftswoman but not everyone is willing to become one. As I walk this earth and city, I find that everyone wants to do what the great ones do but very few are willing to do what they *did* to become great. Too many want five minutes of fame but they don't want to spend the thousands of hours it takes to master their craft.

"When I meet young carpenters they ask me how and why I am in such demand. They think I became an overnight success. But I tell them, there's no such thing as an overnight success. The way to success is the way of the craftsman, where you work really hard for years. You show up every day. You do the work. You see yourself as an artist dedicated to your craft with a desire to get better every day. You put your heart and soul into your work as you strive for excellence. You desire to create perfection, knowing you'll never truly achieve it but hoping to get close to it. You try new things. You fail. You improve. You grow. You face countless challenges and tons of rejection that make you doubt yourself and cause you to want to quit. But you don't. You keep working hard, stay positive, and persevere through it all with resilience, determination, and a lot of hope and faith. Then you make it! Everyone wants to work with you. And the world says, 'Where have you been?' And you say, 'I've been here all along, and hopefully getting better day by day.' To the world, you are an overnight success. To you, the journey continues. You're a craftsman who wants to make your next work of art your best work no matter what you have accomplished in the past." Then he paused and laughed. "Which means your entertainment center is going to be the best work of my life," the carpenter said, smiling as they pulled up to the home improvement store.

Chapter 9

Everybody Loves the Carpenter

It seemed everyone in the store knew the carpenter. As they walked around, one person after another either waved or stopped to say hello to him.

"How you doing, J.?"

"What's going on, J.?"

"How's business, J.?"

"What's your latest project, J.?"

The carpenter waved and said hello to each person and stopped to talk to those who wanted to talk to him. Michael felt like he was walking around with the mayor of home improvement. It seemed everybody loved J. and he loved everybody.

As they drove back to the house, Michael asked, "How do you know all those people?"

"Oh, they were either clients or people I've worked with on various jobs. When you work as long as I have and do as many jobs as I do, you meet a lot of people."

"Meeting a lot of people and having them actually like you and want to spend time with you is another matter altogether," said Michael. "You obviously have a great reputation in the industry. I can see how being a craftsman draws people to you."

"Well, it's more than being a craftsman that draws people to you," said the carpenter. "While I am respected in my industry and stand out from those who merely do work instead of creating art, it is also essential to have the right attitude and approach to your life and work. When you see the good, look for the good, and expect the good, you find the good and the good finds you."

"How so?" asked Michael, who didn't think he was attracting a lot of good lately.

"I don't know how it works exactly," the carpenter said. "I just know that what you think, you become. I know that how you see the world determines the world you see and how the world sees you. I know your perspective can take a bad situation and turn into a great outcome. I know a positive attitude not only draws people to you, but it also gives you power to overcome all the obstacles you will face as you build your success."

"I feel like I'm getting hit with one challenge after another lately," said Michael as they pulled up to his driveway and brought the wood, tools, and materials into the house.

"Yes, you are certainly hitting a rough patch but you're not alone. Anyone who attempts to build great things will face challenges. It's part of the building process. Without struggle there's no reward. Without obstacles there's no growth. Without setbacks there's no triumph. Without failure and defeat along the way there's no ultimate victory and feeling of accomplishment. As a builder of lives and people and teams, you must expect challenges, adversity, rejection, and negativity but have an even greater expectation that you will overcome them."

"I haven't been feeling that way," said Michael. "I guess I've never been in a situation like this before. I used to feel like I was unstoppable. No one had more optimism than me. It's why I wanted to start the business with Sarah. Come on, how many people think they can start a business from nothing and feel like they can make it a household brand? But now I feel like I'm going to be stuck in this house forever. I feel like I've let my wife and family and company down. I'm losing the battle."

"I see it differently," said the carpenter. "I see you resting and learning. I see you getting stronger. I see you preparing for greater things so you can take your life and business to a higher level. Always remember that our biggest battle comes before our greatest victory. And I see great victories in your future."

"I wish I saw what you saw," said Michael, appreciating the encouragement.

"You can! You can *choose* to see it. You can choose to *believe* it. Life and success are about what you choose to believe. It's easy to believe things will be great when everything is going well, but the true test of your faith is what you believe when you are facing seemingly insurmountable challenges. The late and great Nelson Mandela said it best:

> *I am fundamentally an optimist. Whether that comes from nature or nurture, I cannot say. Part of being optimistic is keeping one's head pointed toward the sun, one's feet moving forward.*

*There were many dark moments when
my faith in humanity was sorely tested, but
I would not and could not give myself up
to despair. That way lays defeat and death.*

"And before there was Nelson Mandela there was the greatest carpenter the world has ever known, who said:

"Anything is possible if a person believes."

Chapter 10
Believe

As they cleared the furniture out of the family room and prepared the area to begin their work, the carpenter continued his work on Michael. "We learn best through stories, so let me tell you a story about an ancient tribe that was isolated from the rest of the world. The men in this tribe would run up to 40 miles a day to deliver messages to other tribes. As the men got older, they could actually run faster, longer, and farther than the younger tribesmen. When the researchers found this tribe they were amazed. How could this be, since it went against everything we know and experience in our modern world? In studying and spending time with these people the researchers discovered the secret. It had nothing to do with genes, blood type, or superhuman physical attributes and everything to do with belief. The tribe was isolated from the rest of the world so all they knew was what they saw. What they saw were people running longer, faster, and farther as they got older so this is what they believed to be true. They believed they could run 40 miles a day and so they did."

Then the carpenter put the wood on the floor and turned to Michael, who was listening intently, and said, "When you believe, the impossible becomes possible. What you believe will become what is true. Your optimism today will determine your level of success tomorrow. Don't look at your challenges; look up and look out into the future. Don't focus on your circumstances. Focus on the right beliefs that will help you build your success."

Then the carpenter walked up to Michael, handed him his tool bag, and said, "With these tools you have the power to create, do you not?"

"I do."

"Well, then I want you to think of having the right beliefs as having the tools and the power to create your success. If you say these words each morning when you wake up and throughout the day, you will create an amazing life and know boundless success:

> *I expect great things to happen today.*
>
> *I trust in God's plan for my life.*
>
> *I accept all of the love, joy, abundance, and success in my life.*
>
> *I accept all the people who want to work with me and benefit from my gifts and love.*
>
> *Every day I am getting stronger, healthier, and better.*

"Now repeat after me," he said, and Michael joined him in reciting the phrases.

After a few times Michael stopped and laughed. "I have to tell you, I feel really silly saying these out loud. I feel like I'm at one of those motivational speeches my old company used to send our sales team to. I always felt a little crazy saying them."

"Then don't say them out loud," said the carpenter. "Write them out or say them silently to yourself. If you are not crazy enough to declare what you want to achieve and receive, then you aren't crazy enough to succeed. I don't know if you've realized this or not but you have to be a little crazy to be a big success. Throughout history every genius and great idea has been deemed crazy by those who were too 'normal' to see and understand the 'crazy' person's vision. Small minds can't understand big dreams."

"I guess a lot of people said I was crazy when we started Social Connect," Michael said.

"Of course they did. You were attempting to do what had yet to be done. You have to be a little crazy to want to attempt it, knowing that failure is very likely. And now you have to be a little crazy in your thoughts and beliefs about the future. Don't get normal. Stay crazy. And to do that from now on, I want to encourage you to talk to yourself instead of listening to yourself. It's a powerful tool to build your success."

Chapter 11

Talk to Yourself instead of Listening to Yourself

The carpenter continued. "I once met a man, Dr. James Gills, who completed six double Ironman triathlons. That means he swam for 2.4 miles, rode his bike for 112 miles, and ran 26.2 miles. Then 24 hours later, he did it again. He was the only person on the planet to do this six times. When I asked him how he did it, he paused for a moment and said, 'I have learned to talk to myself instead of listening to myself. If I listen to myself I hear all the negative thoughts, all the complaints, all the fears, all the doubts, and all the reasons why I shouldn't be able to finish the race. But if I talk to myself I can feed myself with the words and encouragement I need to finish the race.' He told me he would memorize and quote scripture, and this kept him going and fueled him toward the finish line.

"How about you? Are you talking to yourself or listening to yourself?" asked the carpenter.

"I've definitely been listening to myself lately."

"And if you were trying to complete an Ironman triathlon with this state of mind, what do you think you would have done by now?"

"I would have given up."

"So what do you need to do from now on?"

"I need to talk to myself and feed myself with the words and encouragement I need to keep moving forward."

"Exactly," said the carpenter as he walked toward the front door to leave, knowing their work was done for the day. "Negative thoughts are the nails that build a prison of failure. Positive thoughts will build you a masterpiece. We are ready for great things. Your mind is prepared for success and the room is prepared for us to begin building our masterpiece tomorrow."

When Michael opened the door and looked outside, he realized the carpenter didn't have a car. "Do you need a ride home?" he asked.

"No, I love to walk. Gives me time to think, reflect, imagine, and create beautiful things," he said before flashing his radiant smile and giving Michael a hug. Then before he left he handed Michael a card from his pocket. "Here, take this. It's a positive pledge that you can say when challenges come your way and you aren't feeling very positive." Michael looked at the card. It said:

I vow to stay positive in the face of negativity.

When I am surrounded by pessimism, I will choose optimism.

When I feel fear, I will choose faith.

When I want to hate, I will choose love.

When I want to be bitter, I will choose to get better.

When I experience a challenge, I will look for an opportunity to learn and grow.

When faced with adversity, I will find strength.

When I experience a setback, I will be resilient.

When I meet failure, I will fail forward, toward future success.

With vision, hope, and faith, I will never give up and will always move forward toward my destiny.

I believe my best days are ahead of me, not behind me.

I believe I'm here for a reason and my purpose is greater than my challenges.

I believe that being positive not only makes me better, it makes everyone around me better.

So today and every day I will be positive and strive to make a positive impact on the world.

Michael closed the door, walked inside, stood in the family room, and looked at all the wood and materials. It seemed like a mess, much like his life, but for the first time since his accident he had a glimmer of hope and belief that it was all going to come together.

Unfortunately, that night he would need to read the positive pledge and talk to himself more than ever because he was about to receive some bad news.

Chapter 12

Sarah

When people called them a power couple Michael knew it was because of Sarah. She was the strongest and most positive woman he had ever known and the glue that kept their family together. They met on a sales call years before and, for him, it was love at first sight. For her, it took a few years. When she finally let her guard down and opened her heart to him, Michael, being the salesman he was, made her an offer that turned out to be the best sale of his life. Over the years Sarah's strength and resolve never wavered as they built a house, a marriage, a family, and now a business together. But for the first time she seemed fearful. Building a house didn't scare her. Giving birth without drugs, *twice*, didn't scare her. Even putting everything they owned into their new business didn't scare her. But ever since that day in the hospital, she was fearful of losing Michael, and when she walked in the door from work that night, she looked like someone had died.

She didn't want to tell him. In fact, she tried not to but couldn't hide her despair. Michael made her talk and she shared that they had lost their biggest client. The contract would run for two more months, but then they were done.

"I knew I shouldn't have taken time off," Michael yelled.

"It wasn't because you took time off," she said, trying to calm him down. "It was because of our service. We didn't serve the account well enough. We grew too fast beyond our ability to serve the client. You know it was something we talked a lot about. We feared this would happen and it did."

"I need to come back tomorrow," he said.

"No, you aren't!" she yelled as the kids walked out from the rooms where they were doing homework.

"What's the matter?" their daughter asked as their son started to cry.

"I have to go think," Michael said as he walked to his office and shut the door before falling to the floor and lying down on his back. The first image he saw was a CLOSED sign on their office door and a FORECLOSED sign on their front lawn. This was their biggest client. How could they survive without them? He didn't have an answer. For the first time in his life he didn't have a solution. For the first time in years, he started to cry. He knew he wasn't strong enough to get through this on his own. He would need to find a different source of strength to overcome this. "What do I do now?" he shouted as he looked up to the ceiling. "Help me. Please give me strength!"

In that moment a feeling of peace came over him and ideas started to flood his mind. He was filled with the belief that everything happens for a reason and good things would come from this. He began talking to himself, remembering the encouraging words his older brother George used to say to him. George had met a bus driver who changed his life, and ever since he would call Michael once in a while to talk and share a positive message with him. Michael looked at the positive pledge on his desk and gathered himself. About 10 minutes later he walked outside to where Sarah was sitting at the table. She was shocked when he said, "Our purpose is greater than our challenges. This happened for a reason. It's going to make us better and stronger in the future. We've been relying on this one big client for too long and it just means we have to find more clients to spread out our business and our risk. We'll begin tomorrow when I come back to the office."

"I agree with you about everything except the part where you are coming back tomorrow," Sarah said with such resolve that Michael knew it would be hard to argue with her. "I'd rather lose the business than you. You can come back in a week. One more week to rest and recharge and then you can come back. We still have two more months before the contract ends. I can work to improve customer service immediately and talk to our sales team, and when you come back you can focus on getting a few clients to keep us above water. You'll have plenty of time."

"Fine," said Michael sheepishly. He didn't agree with her but figured even he could do a week. Besides he was thrilled she said only a week. He thought she was going to make him stay away for a month.

"There's just one caveat," Sarah said. "You have to see the doctor first and get some tests done before you come back. Deal?"

"Deal," Michael said, knowing he was being outsold by a techie. "I'll even go see the dentist and get a root canal if it means I can start selling again." Nothing was going to stop him from coming back to work. In the meantime he was going to research potential clients he could sell and close quickly. His family, his business, and his future depended on it.

Chapter 13

Chaos

Michael and Sarah were running around the house trying to get the kids ready for school when the doorbell rang. Sarah opened the door and the carpenter was standing there with his tool box in one hand and a handcrafted wooden heart in the other.

"Hi, I'm J. Emmanuel," he said cheerfully and handed Sarah the heart, freeing up his hand so he could shake hers. "I made this for your family."

"Thank you! What a beautiful gift," she said, trying to act calm amid the morning craziness. "But I'm the one who should be giving you a gift. You saved my husband's life and I can't thank you enough."

"Oh, it was nothing. It was my pleasure, and I'm just glad we are starting to build something great together. Do you mind if I get started? I know it's early but I wanted to get a good start since there's a lot to do today."

"No, that's fine. Come on in," said Sarah as they walked to the family room and Michael walked out of the kids' rooms with clothes in one hand, a backpack in the other.

"Hey, J. Great to see you," he said, not really meaning it. "You're here early, huh?"

"I know, I know, I just wanted to get an early start today. I'll come later from now on but today there's a lot to do."

"That's fine; whatever works," said Michael, although he was glad J. wouldn't make this a habit. "We just have to get the kids ready for school so feel free to do whatever you need to do. There's water in the fridge and I'll join you soon."

For the next 20 minutes Michael and Sarah frantically scrambled around the house trying to get the kids out the door on time to make the bus. They, along with the kids, waved and said hi each time they dashed passed the family room while the carpenter just smiled and waved back. When the kids had finally made their bus, Sarah walked back to the house with her husband and thanked the carpenter once again for saving his life before leaving for work. After she left, Michael just plopped down onto the couch in the family room and took a deep breath.

"Now I can see why you passed out on your run," the carpenter said, laughing but also stating the truth.

"Tell me about it. That's not even the half of it," Michael said before telling him about last night and losing their biggest client. "I feel like I'm on a runaway train heading toward a cliff and there's nothing I can do to stop it. I can't tell if I'm racing to the top or the bottom, if you know what I mean."

"I understand," said the carpenter. "But you're not alone. It seems all my clients and everyone I meet these days feel the same way. They are being bombarded with challenges and dealing with such busyness and stress that they can't even think straight. It's like the new plague of our day. Those who can manage it will thrive. Those who don't will perish."

"We'll I'm definitely on my way to perishing," said Michael before realizing he was listening to himself instead of talking to himself.

"It doesn't have to be this way," the carpenter said. "There's another way, or what I call *The Way*, if you want to know what it is."

"Of course," said Michael. "My way is definitely not working."

Chapter 14

The Greatest Success Strategy of All

"Well then, let me tell you about *The Way*," the carpenter said. "But first I must tell you what gets in the way. It is *fear*. Truth be told, the root cause of busyness and stress is fear. The stress you are experiencing at work and home are manifestations of the fear that is driving you. I bet when you were starting out you had all sorts of self-esteem issues and fears. You had fears that you weren't good enough, smart enough, or fortunate enough to be successful. This fear pushed you to work hard and conquer your demons. And you had some success, right?"

"Yes," Michael said while nodding.

"But with that success more fears emerged. People think the more successful you become the less fear you have. But actually you often become more fearful. You don't want to lose what you have built. More people are looking to you and at you so you feel more pressure. You feel you have more to prove and more to lose. The success is greater, so the fall is greater if you fail, and too often the fear of failure becomes a self-fulfilling prophecy that leads to failure. That's why I always told my children *do not fear* knowing that fear was the one thing that would keep them from their destiny. Does this sound about right?" he asked.

"Yes," said Michael. "All of it." His self-esteem had never been lower and his fear had never been greater. "It's like you are reading my mind."

The carpenter picked up the wooden heart and showed it to Michael. "You collapsed not because there was something wrong with your heart but because of the fear that was in your heart. The great news is there is an answer and it is the most powerful medicine in the world.

"*The Way* begins with love and love is the antidote to the fear, busyness, and stress you feel," he said. Then he paused, thought for a moment and continued, "Do not fear failing. Do not fear losing clients. Do not fear that you won't be successful. Do not fear that things won't go your way. Instead do everything with love and you will cast out fear, you will flow instead of stress, and you will create more success than you could ever imagine."

"Easier said than done," said Michael. "My fear hovers around me, latches on like a pit bull, and won't let go."

"I know," said the carpenter. "But that's why I call it *The Way*. It's the way to live each moment, each day to the fullest, and prevent all the negative forces from sabotaging you. The more you focus on love in each moment and each day, the more fear fades away.

"Think of the craftsman beginning a new work. The craftsman is not thinking about failure. The craftsman is only thinking about building his work with love. Because he loves his work so much and creates with love, fear loses its power over the craftsman. And this allows him to do his best work and create with all the love in the universe.

"You thought you were a craftsman, didn't you, Michael?" the carpenter asked.

"I did. When you were describing a craftsman, I kept saying to myself, 'That's me.' I work harder than anyone I know. I'm always trying to get better. I pursue excellence in all that I do. But . . ."

"But," the carpenter interrupted and completed his sentence, "you are missing the love the craftsman creates with. You cannot be a craftsman unless you are putting your love into the work that you do. After all, if you aren't building it with love it won't be worth building. As an artist you must be driven by love. Only then will you create something special, magnificent, and compelling. Only through love will you create a masterpiece."

Michael knew he was right. He was building with fear and it almost cost him his life.

The carpenter continued, "If you build your life and company with fear, it won't be worth building. In the end you'll look back and realize you didn't enjoy any of it. It will never be what it could have been and you'll likely burn out before you finish. And even if you do finish, anything built with fear will eventually crumble."

"Like my collapse," said Michael.

"Exactly like that. Remember, fear is draining. Love is sustaining. Fear is short term. Love is long term. Fear appears strong, but is weak. Love appears weak, but is strong. Love is the way."

The carpenter then held the wooden heart against his heart before handing it to Michael, who asked, "How do I make *The Way* my way?"

"It's simple," the carpenter said. "When it comes to your business, focus on the love you have of building it rather than the fear of losing it. Don't let fear sabotage your dreams. You only have one life to live so you might as well go for it. Fill it up with love, not fear. When you build your business with love, it can't help but grow. When you love the work you do, you will do great work. You were created with love, you are loved, and you are meant to share this love in all that you do. Build everything with love! Greatness is built with love."

The carpenter then walked toward Michael's children's rooms, turned around, and smiled. "And when you are getting your children ready for school in the morning, for God's sake, love the time you have with them instead of fearing you won't make the bus. You all will be a lot happier," he said laughing.

"Well said!" Michael exclaimed, knowing it was the truth he needed to hear. "But what about all the obstacles and annoying little things that get in the way? Like shoelaces and book reports and losing your most important client?" he said sarcastically.

"They are like barking dogs that are powerless in the face of love," answered the carpenter. "All those things are opportunities to choose how you want to live. In every moment will you choose fear or love? Choose love and:

Love the struggle because it makes you
appreciate your accomplishments.
Love challenges because they make you stronger.

Love competition because it makes you better.

Love negative people because they make you more positive.

Love those who have hurt you because they teach you forgiveness.

Love fear because it makes you courageous.

"The secret to life and the greatest success strategy of all is to love all of it and fear none of it."

Chapter 15

Love Is a Commitment

That night Michael sat in his office and thought about what the carpenter said and what it was like as they walked around the home improvement store together. He realized all those people weren't drawn to J. just because he was great at his work. They were drawn to him because he loved his work and that's what made him great. They also loved him because he exuded love in everything he did.

Michael had never thought of love as a strategy but now realized how it was missing from his work and business. He had stopped loving his business and started to fear it. He had stopped loving his work and started to dread it. When you love something that love shines through in everything you do and everything you create. He knew that at one point in his career but had stopped living it because of the stress, busyness, and fear that caused him to worry about the outcome instead of loving the journey.

He picked up a book from his desk that Sarah had bought him a few days after he got out of the hospital. The book talked about how busyness and stress are the enemies of great leadership, teamwork, customer service, and careers. It said that science tells us when we are busy and stressed we activate the reptilian part of our brain. This is significant because reptiles do not make decisions based on love. They are all about survival. If they are hungry they will eat you, not love you like the family dog would. They make decisions based on fear and survival. And so do humans when we feel busy and stressed. Loving others is the last thing on our mind when we are stressed. Instead the reptilian part of our brain is thinking about how to just make it through the day, and it will eat anyone for lunch that gets in its way. The book then went on to say that the good news, however, is that we have another part of the brain called the neocortex. The author called it the Positive Dog part of our brain (because of the loving nature of dogs) and we activate it when we love, care, pray, and practice gratitude. In any moment we can override the reptile with the positive dog. We can choose to love people instead of ignoring them. We can choose to slow down instead of rushing. We can choose to be intentional rather than reactionary. And we can take some deep breaths, focus on love and gratitude, and change how we approach the day and the people in our lives.

That's why the carpenter said do everything with love and gratitude, Michael thought as he looked over at the family dog, Matt, who was lying on the floor at his feet, looking up at him. He thought it was funny they had a dog named Matt but that's what the rescue shelter said his name was and it stuck. Ever since they brought him home, he had been the most loving dog they ever had. He was the first to greet Michael when he walked in the door. He hung out with him in his office and relished their walks together. Yet, in reading this book, Michael realized that he ignored Matt too much. Too many times he wanted to stop and rub his belly but his reptilian brain would tell him to keep moving, hurry up, eat breakfast, and ignore the dog. Matt would look at him with his big eyes and loving face as if to say, "Love me; it will benefit you more than me," but Michael didn't and he felt sad about it.

Michael's life was based on fear, not love. He knew he needed to change and would start right now. He sat down on the floor and rubbed Matt's belly. He realized that love isn't just a feeling. It is a commitment. After all you don't always feel capable of loving. You don't always feel loving toward your family, especially when they are stressing you out. You certainly don't always feel like you love your team. You don't always feel like taking the time to show others you love them. Loving others is not always convenient or comfortable. Choosing to love, then, meant you were choosing to make a commitment that you will love regardless of how you feel and you will put love into action regardless of your circumstances.

Michael continued to pet Matt. No longer would he ignore him. No longer would he allow busyness, stress, and fear to keep him from loving those he was committed to. He would choose love instead of fear and do everything with love. He would do a better job of loving his team and he would help his company do a better job of loving their clients. The carpenter called it *The Way* and Michael decided from now on it would be the way he would lead his company and the way his company approached their clients. Yes, love wouldn't only be a great success strategy for him as a leader. It would be a great strategy for his company, especially in sales and customer service. Now he just had to figure out how they would put love into action so they could keep the clients they had and get a few more clients they needed.

Chapter 16
People > Furniture

The next morning the house was quiet. Sarah and the kids were gone. The only sounds Michael heard were a lawn mower next door and the carpenter measuring a piece of wood. Michael shared his thoughts about love being a commitment and J. passionately added that it was also an investment. "When you love someone or something, you make the time to invest in it. I love everything I make, so I put all my love into it. It's the same with relationships. We are meant to love others by investing in them. Unfortunately in today's world, I see far too many people investing in things more than relationships. Even though I'm a carpenter I know people are more important than furniture," he said as he measured another piece of wood.

Michael smiled but then searched his heart and discovered he was guilty of not investing more in his own relationships. At home he did a much better job than at work but still fell short, and with his daughter's youth basketball team, he realized he needed to improve a lot.

The carpenter continued, "I tell everyone who will listen that even though I'm known for sharing success strategies, true success isn't about money or possessions. It's about people, commitment, loyalty, and relationships. In the end we won't be measured by our bank accounts, sales numbers, wins and losses, or the size of the company we built, but by the difference we made in people's lives—and we make a difference through relationships. So don't be so busy chasing dollars and success that you fail to make a difference and build meaningful relationships."

As Michael listened to the carpenter all he could say was "I know. I know. I know." He realized he was guilty of focusing more on building his business than his relationships. He saw every client as an opportunity to build up himself and his business rather than just building a solid relationship like he used to do when he was in sales at his old company.

The carpenter knew exactly how Michael's mind worked. He had worked with many clients just like him and noticed all too often that the more successful someone became, the more their relationships suffered. Everyone was so busy trying to make money they forgot that life is about people, not things. The carpenter knew what Michael needed to hear and continued sharing. He said, "Invest in relationships, not because you want something, but because you want to build something! Ironically when you focus on making a difference and building relationships, success will find you."

"I want to make this a priority with my team when I get back to work," said Michael.

"That's great, because if you want to build your company, you must build your people. Invest in them and build them up, and they will love coming to work and will perform at a higher level. If you grow them as people, they will grow your company.

"It also works the same way with customers. If you want to build your company, love your customers and invest in a relationship with them. When you love your customers, they will multiply," the carpenter said as he walked over to the plant by the window and held it up. "All things grow with love."

Then he continued, "It works most powerfully with families. I tell people all the time that if you want to build your family, you must take the time to invest in your marriage and kids. I know you are really good about investing in your family but as your success builds remember to not ignore those who are closest to you. No one does this on purpose but the busier we get, the more our priorities get out of whack. Slowly and subtly we spend less time and communicate less with those who will be crying at our funeral and before we know it, we look around and we're alone and feel empty. So make sure you continually identify the relationships in your life that need to be stronger and then make a conscious effort to focus on them, make time for them, develop them, and invest in them. If we make time to invest in our relationships and spend quality time with our family, friends, and colleagues, we will dramatically improve the quality of our lives and careers. I believe we are who we are because someone loved us. And your team and family will become who they become because you love them."

Chapter 17

The Second Greatest Success Strategy of All

"How do I put love into action? What's the best way to show I'm committed and invested?" asked Michael, who had been thinking about it all the previous night.

"Well," said the carpenter, "the answer to your question happens to be the next success strategy I want to share with you. But before I share this strategy, can you get me a glass of water? I'm very thirsty." Michael ran to the kitchen, poured him a cup of water, and brought it to him. The carpenter chugged it down in one giant gulp before asking Michael to get him a shrimp burrito from his favorite place. "I forgot my lunch today and am going to be very hungry at noon. I do my best work with a happy belly and my belly is happiest with shrimp burritos," he said.

Michael thought it was a strange request since it was a few hours before noon but he ran to the burrito shop, which served breakfast and lunch burritos, and bought a few for the carpenter and himself. He sat in traffic for a while because a car was stuck in the road and he had to navigate a bunch of side roads to get home.

When he finally arrived home, the carpenter was outside in the backyard cutting the wood pieces that would make up the main part of the entertainment center. As soon as Michael walked outside, the carpenter asked, "Can you grab that piece of wood over there?" Michael brought over the wood and J. told him to place it on top of the other pieces. When they finished cutting the pieces he directed Michael to grab the sander and help him sand the surface of each piece of wood. Then, he asked Michael to get the screwdriver and screws and bring them over to him. When they were finished he asked Michael to go get him another glass of water. When Michael returned with the water, the carpenter said, "And now you drink it."

"Ok," said Michael before taking a sip. "But why did you ask me to get it for you then?"

"Because I wanted to demonstrate the second greatest strategy of all to you," he said. "So far I have shared several of my favorite success strategies. Love, of course, being the greatest of them all. Love then leads us to the second greatest strategy of all and it is to *serve*. All morning, you did things to serve me and didn't even think about it. You didn't question when I asked you to get me another cup of water. You wanted to serve in order to help. You weren't thinking about yourself. You were thinking about me and the work I was doing. You were serving from the heart."

Then they walked inside and the carpenter grabbed the wooden heart he had made and took out a sharp tool and carved the word *Love*, then added *Serve* underneath. "Because we love, we serve. And when we serve others, we fill up their cup with love and our own as well."

Michael looked pensively at the words on the heart as he thought about what the carpenter was saying and his own experiences. "But serving gets exhausting," said Michael, who was thinking about how he felt the last few months trying to help his family, employees, customers, and his daughter's youth basketball team.

"It gets tiring if you serve out of fear," the carpenter said. "But if you serve with love, as you did today, it's actually energizing. People think they will get tired if they serve too much, but that's not how service works. When you serve with love and refresh others, you too will be refreshed."

Michael took another sip of the water and realized the water he brought for J. was now filling him up.

"Don't let the fear of getting tired get in the way of serving others," the carpenter continued. "And don't let fear, busyness, and stress keep you from serving with love. Because of fear, most people in leadership positions become self-serving. They try to accumulate power by protecting and serving themselves. But real leaders, great leaders, become powerful by serving others and giving their power away with love. Only by serving can you become truly great! Do you know why that is?" he asked as he handed Michael the wooden heart.

"I'm not sure," Michael said as his memory flashed back to his high school and college summers in the northeast when he would lifeguard at the beach. The head lifeguard called his job an act of service, but Michael didn't think much about it at the time.

"Well then, let me ask you another question. Tell me some of the greatest leaders throughout history. Who do we admire the most?"

Michael thought for a little while and rattled off a few names. "Gandhi, Martin Luther King, Jr., Jesus, Abraham Lincoln, George Washington."

"Good list," the carpenter said. "And why do we honor those who served in our military on Veterans Day and Memorial Day?"

"Because they served and sacrificed," Michael said as he looked at the wooden heart and remembered the time he saved an elderly woman from drowning in a strong undertow during his first year of lifeguarding.

"Yes!" the carpenter exclaimed. "When you love, you serve, and when you serve, you sacrifice. Service requires a sacrifice of something. Whether it's time, energy, money, love, effort, or focus, serving others always costs you something, but with service and sacrifice, you gain so much more. We admire those who serve and sacrifice for us and others admire us for our service and sacrifice. There is nothing more powerful than sacrificial love. Nothing says I love you more than letting someone know I am willing to serve and sacrifice for them. When you love and serve others you will become great in their eyes. They will know you love them and they will love you back. They will respect and honor you. They will trust you. They will tell others about you. Serving leads to true success."

"You can't fake it, either," said Michael as he remembered a boss who pretended to love and serve, but everyone knew he was full of it.

"No, you can't fake it. You can't pretend to serve your way to power. Some try to but it doesn't last. We know who would run into a burning building to save us. Truth shines through. Those who serve to gain power don't last. Those who serve and give their power away receive power from those they serve. That's why when you serve in small ways you get more opportunities to serve in big ways. That's why when you start serving the few it leads to serving the many.

"That's why the greatest leader the world has ever known wasn't a dictator. He was a servant who came to serve and wash feet. That's why we honor Martin Luther King, Jr. and Gandhi. They gave their lives for a cause greater than themselves. Their sacrifice was our gain. We became better people in a better world because of them. We don't love and admire the tyrant, the prideful, or the arrogant. We love and honor the humble servant who loves us and makes us better.

"Always remember that your greatness as a leader will not be determined by how much power you accumulate. It will be determined by how much you serve and sacrifice for others to help them become great. Great leaders don't succeed because they are great. They succeed because they bring out the greatness in others. I believe you have to have an ego to want to be great but ironically you must give up your ego and serve others in order to be great. To become a great leader, you must be a servant leader. Only through service and sacrifice do you become great. You must serve in order to lead."

"How do I become a servant leader?" asked Michael as a million thoughts raced overwhelmingly through this mind.

"It's simple," said the carpenter. "When you get back to work, I want to encourage you to look for opportunities to serve others as you served me today. As you served me all morning, serve your team. Ask your employees what they need and serve them. Anticipate their needs and serve them before they even know they need it. Ask your customers what they need from you to be their best. Anticipate and serve their needs as well. The greatest salespeople succeed because they love and serve their clients. It's also important to teach your team to serve each other. Great teammates serve the team more than themselves. When a team is more committed to serving one another rather than their own selfish desires, they become very powerful and accomplish amazing things."

Michael took a deep breath as he looked at the words on the wooden heart. He couldn't argue with the carpenter. Just as the words were carved in the wood, their truth was being engraved in his own heart. Love was a commitment and an investment, and he needed to do a better job of serving others more than himself. He had thought he was serving but now he realized he was just leading out of fear, which drained him. Now he knew serving with love was what he needed to do to sustain him and his company. He had saved lives as a lifeguard, and now he needed to save his own life and his company with the same approach to service and sacrifice.

"You know there's one more strategy to add to the heart," the carpenter said as he reached out his hand and pointed to the spot under the words *Love* and *Serve*. "It's the third greatest success strategy of all and it completes the greatest, simplest, most powerful success model of all."

"What is it?" asked Michael, hoping it would give him more ideas and practical strategies to implement when he went back to work.

"I will share it with you tomorrow. It's important to slowly digest each of these three strategies and think about how you will implement them. Besides, right now I would love to eat and digest a burrito."

It was noon and the carpenter was hungry.

Chapter 18

The Sandwich

After a productive day of measuring, sawing, sanding, and building, the carpenter went to the burrito shop to meet potential clients who wanted to hire him, while Michael drove his daughter to basketball practice. Sarah had given him the okay to help the other coaches, but he wasn't allowed to lead the practice or yell.

On the way, Michael thought about the first and greatest coach he ever had, his mother. He remembered visiting her seven years ago and taking a walk together. She was a walking machine who walked for miles every day, but on this day she seemed very tired. Michael tried to convince her to turn around but she wouldn't listen. She wanted to walk with him to the grocery store so they could get ingredients for her to make him a sandwich for his five-hour drive home. They made it to the grocery store, but on the way back she grew more and more tired. When they got back to her place, Michael told her to go rest and take a nap, but she wouldn't. She walked right into the kitchen and made him a sandwich.

On his way home he ate that sandwich but didn't think much about it at the time. Now seven years later, he thought about that sandwich in a whole new way. On that day his mom was dying from cancer but hadn't told him how bad it was. She took a quick turn for the worse and that was the last time he saw her alive. Here she was, battling cancer, and her biggest priority was to make him a sandwich.

She not only encouraged him and pushed him to be his best but she modeled the ultimate act of love and service for him. She put him first when she should have put herself first. He knew his mom would run into a burning building to save him, and she was the reason why he would run into the ocean to save an elderly woman at the beach. She was a great coach who taught him to love and serve. As he looked out the window and thought about the sandwich, he realized that serving isn't always about big sacrifices and huge acts of service. It's about doing little things each day to show people you love and care about them. It's about doing small acts with a big heart and a big dose of love.

That night at practice Michael focused on loving and serving his daughter's teammates. He focused on helping them get better. He stopped thinking about winning and beating the other team and started building each girl up with positive words of encouragement and simple tips to help them get better.

He didn't yell once and even his daughter commented that it was the best practice of the year. He was beginning to understand *The Way*. Now he just had to figure out how to do this with his company, because they were drowning and needed someone to save them.

Chapter 19

The Third Greatest Success Strategy of All

The next day the carpenter wisely showed up after Sarah and the kids were gone, and proceeded to build the entertainment center with Michael. They were building the back of it and, of course, the carpenter used the finest wood available. While taking a short break, he grabbed the heart and carved the word *Care* underneath *Serve* before showing the heart to Michael.

"This is the third greatest success strategy of all," he said passionately. "It's my favorite to talk about because when you care about the work you do and show people you care about them, you stand out in a world where most don't care. Caring leads to success!"

"If there's one thing I know about myself," said Michael, "it's that I care a lot."

"And it shows," said the carpenter. "The fact that you care so much is why I care to share these strategies with you. Caring draws people to you. We all want to work with people who care. We want to help people who care. When you care, you attract people like a magnet. You asked me the other day why all those people wanted to talk to me at the store, and it is because I'm a craftsman with a positive attitude who loves, serves, and cares.

"If you want to be successful you must show you care about the work that you do. I care about what I build and people can see this care in my work. That's why people come to meet me and hire me, even when I'm not able to return voicemails. They know I care about my work, and it is the best marketing strategy of all," he said as Michael smiled. He had come to realize the carpenter was a better marketer than he had thought.

"The world knows when someone cares, don't they?" Michael asked, realizing in that moment that Social Connect had lost its biggest client because they had become too big too fast and didn't care enough.

"Without a doubt. The world will flock to people who care and buy products that were made with care and support businesses that care, like my favorite burrito shop. I can tell with each burrito whether the person making it cared enough to make it great. I can tell whether the person working at the register actually cares about people or is just there to collect a paycheck. If people there stop caring about their work and me, I'll find a new place that does care."

"I know what you mean," said Michael. "My wife stopped going to this popular hair salon because they stopped caring about her. They got very busy and became more commercial and less caring. Now, she's looking for another place that will care about her."

"Well that's just it," the carpenter said, waving his hands passionately. "When you care, you not only care about the work that you do, but you also show people you care about them. When you care, everyone matters and everything matters."

The carpenter put his hand at the top of the entertainment center and with an open palm gently moved his hand slowly toward the bottom, caressing it like he would his child's hair. "When we care, we care about every inch, every detail. We care about design. We care about the materials we use. We care about ingredients. We care about our team. We care about each interaction. We care about how each team member feels. We care about service. We care about how each customer feels. We care about all the little things that lead to big success. When we care, we build things that others care about. When we care, we are craftsmen and craftswomen who are always looking to get better, work harder, and care more."

Michael and the carpenter then exchanged stories of their favorite businesses that understood the power of caring. They talked about the supermarket that trains their employees to take you to the item on the shelf when you can't find what you are looking for, the tire center employees that run and greet their customers as soon as they arrive, the company that provides free shipping and free returns, the airline that cares about their employees and customers so much that LUV is their stock symbol, and the restaurants that go out of their way to accommodate people with food allergies, like Michael's children. Michael's favorite example of caring was Fitz, who works at Rosenblum's, and sells Michael his suits. "Every time I put on a new suit or pair of pants for the first time, I find an encouraging message from Fitz on a notecard tucked into a pocket. It's not a note thanking me for his business, but a note that makes me smile, laugh, and enjoy the rest of the day. One time I was about to meet with an important client and felt a card in the inside pocket of my new jacket. I pulled out the card and it was a note from Fitz that said, *Your day just got a whole lot better*. I love that he takes the time to write a handwritten note that lifts me up. He cares, and I wouldn't think of buying my clothes anywhere else."

The carpenter responded, "Fitz clearly understands *The Way* and has found a unique way to show he cares. It may seem like a small gesture but it means everything. Over the years I've discovered that the most successful people, companies, and organizations stand out by finding unique ways to show they care and they make it a habit. For me it's about the work I do; for another business it might be that they are available and responsive to their customers' needs 24/7. Some may even show they care by returning voicemails faster than their competition. The key is to find the unique way that fits you and your work."

Michael and the carpenter then discussed how caring is the differentiator in every profession, and agreed that the best sports teams are composed of players who care not only about being their best but also care about their teammates. They discussed their school experiences and realized their favorite teachers and coaches were the ones who cared about them. Michael commented how a caring doctor and nurse had made all the difference when he was in the hospital. They agreed that those who care go out of their way to make others feel important.

Then the carpenter said, "Always remember that great organizations that care are composed of people who care greatly—and it starts with you. Not because you are the leader of the company, but because one person who cares inspires everyone around them to care. Anyone in any organization can be a CCO, Chief Caring Officer."

Michael laughed. "I think I was the CCO in the last company I worked for," he said. "I don't think I was the best salesperson from a technique standpoint. But I won all the awards because I found out what the customer really wanted and I cared about them and made sure they got what they wanted. I didn't try to sell them something they didn't need."

"Did other people follow your lead?" asked the carpenter.

"Yes, they did. I believe we became a more successful sales team and organization because my caring rubbed off on others."

"That's the secret to building a great organization and team," the carpenter said. "When you care, you will inspire others to care. It's also important to make sure you surround yourself with people who care. Then, together you take action to show you care. Find ways to extend yourself to others and serve them. Write a note. Make a call. Go out of your way to serve someone. Go beyond the expected. People know you care when you go out of your way to show them they matter. A smile, an encouraging word, an extra five minutes of time, solving a customer's problem, listening to an employee, sacrificing for a friend, and helping a team member through a challenging time can make all the difference. Never underestimate the importance of making time to make someone feel special.

"Then when you develop a reputation for caring and others expect more from you, you continue to deliver more than they expect. With each caring act you are saying, 'I am here to love you and serve you,' and when this happens, you attract more love. They will talk about you and refer you. They will tell stories at parties and gatherings about you. People may even write books about you. Caring is the ultimate success building strategy. People make it complicated but it's simple:

> Care about the work you do.
>
> Surround yourself with people who care.
>
> Show your team you care about them.
>
> Build a team that cares about one another.
>
> Together show your customers you care about them.

"This is how you stand out and succeed."

Chapter 20

Love, Serve, Care

The carpenter could tell Michael was in deep thought. "What's troubling you?" he asked.

"I'm not troubled. I'm just thinking about ways to put all of this into action when I get back to work in a few days."

The carpenter showed Michael the wooden heart. "It's as simple as this: You love, you serve, and you show people you care. It's the simplest, most powerful, greatest success model of all time. You take the three words on this heart and you put them on your heart. When you are leading your team, you love, serve, and care. When you sell, you love, serve, and care. When you coach and mentor, you love, serve, and care. When you serve your customers, you love, serve, and care. You implement *The Way* individually and collectively, and you will be successful in all that you do.

"Then you share this model with your team by modeling it for them. If you want your team to love, you love them. If you want them to serve, you serve them. If you want them to care, you care about them. If you want them to give their best, you give them your best. It doesn't happen overnight but the work you put in today becomes the masterpiece you enjoy tomorrow.

"Then you ingrain this model into the people around you by encouraging each of them to identify and internalize what it means to love, serve, and care. It can't exist as just words on a piece of wood. It must come alive in the hearts and minds of all who work with you. Everyone can choose to love, serve, and care and when they do, they will become leaders of others. Not all leaders love, serve, and care, but all who love, serve, and care are leaders.

"In this spirit it's important for you and your team to find every opportunity to put this model into practice to lead others. I believe we possess the greatest power in the universe, the power to make a difference in the life of another human being. If we lived and shared this model, it would not only transform our businesses, schools, and teams but also the world."

The carpenter smiled, handed Michael the wooden heart, and said, "Speaking of putting this model into practice, can you love, serve, and care by going to get us some shrimp burritos while I stain the wood? Our masterpiece is almost finished."

Chapter 21

Value

The next morning as the carpenter was putting the final touches on his masterpiece, Michael wrote him a check. He decided to pay him more than what J. had quoted him. The carpenter didn't just talk about loving, serving, and caring; he lived those words, and that increased his value tenfold. He wasn't just a carpenter. He was a teacher, mentor, and coach who loved, served, and cared about Michael.

Michael realized that when you love, serve, and care it shows you value others and, in turn, your value to the world increases. For the first time, he realized the time away from work had been good for him. He needed to heal his heart so he could give all of it to his team. The carpenter had showed him *The Way* and Michael was ready to improve the way he lived, led, and worked. He was both excited and nervous about going back to work. He had a powerful model to share, but he wondered if there would be enough time to share it before their biggest client was officially gone. Could he acquire a few more clients? Could they improve customer service quickly enough? Could he stay calm and healthy in the process?

The carpenter walked over and stood next to Michael as they looked at the entertainment center. It was the most magnificent work of craftsmanship Michael had ever seen. It was absolutely beautiful. Michael called it a work of art. Now if he could just use the carpenter's success strategies to build his business into a masterpiece.

When they made their way to the front door, Michael didn't wait for J. to hug him; he hugged the carpenter.

"I can't thank you enough," he said. "For everything!"

"Let me know how it goes when you get back to work," the carpenter said. "You have my number."

"I'll leave you a voicemail because I know you won't answer the phone," Michael said smiling.

"Don't expect a call back," the carpenter said before letting out a hearty laugh.

"I won't," said Michael. "But I'll know where to find you if I need to talk."

"Sounds like a plan." The carpenter knew they would be talking soon. All of his clients came to see him shortly after learning his strategies. Michael was equipped with the greatest success strategies of all, and with them came incredible power and also big challenges.

"I'll see you soon," J. said before walking outside and down the road as he headed to his next job, where he would create another masterpiece.

Chapter 22

The Heart of Success

For the next few days Michael loved, served, and cared at home and at his daughter's basketball practices. He had a few more days until he returned to work but at least he was able to put the strategies to the test with his family and nine-year-old girls playing basketball. Each morning he talked to himself instead of listened to himself, and while taking a slow walk in the park, he recited the phrases the carpenter had taught him. His wife commented on how much more calm he seemed while getting the kids ready for school. She also loved the fact that he was helping out by doing laundry and vacuuming the house.

The kids loved that he started writing positive messages on their brown lunch bags and on whiteboards in their rooms. He took the carpenter's words to heart and decided that, for good or for bad, we all share and reinforce beliefs and messages that become part of how our children think and what they believe. Instead of giving them the *curse* of pessimism, cynicism, and negativity, he decided he would give them the *gift* of encouragement, optimism, and belief. He wanted to create the pathway to their future accomplishments, victories, and triumphs with the right belief system and so he wrote a positive message each day.

His doctor noticed a difference in him, too. Michael's medical tests and blood work showed no concerns whatsoever and he was given a clean bill of health. In fact, his blood pressure was lower and all his numbers were better than before his fall. The doctor said, "Whatever you are doing, keep doing it. It's working." Michael gave him a spontaneous hug, knowing this meant he could go back to work. He sprinted out of the building to his car, feeling better and stronger than ever.

He told Sarah about the good news from the doctor and everything he had learned from the carpenter. While she was surprised that he would learn so much from a guy who built entertainment centers, she didn't care how he got better. She was just thankful he was better. The positive changes at home and his clean bill of health convinced her to not only allow him to go back to work but to also return as head coach of their daughter's basketball team for the upcoming game. She figured it would be a good test to see how he responded in a stressful situation.

That weekend Michael saw the first fruit of putting Love, Serve, Care into practice. His daughter's basketball team, which was the worst in the league and had lost every game they played, finally had their first win. The other team's coach commented that there was a noticeable difference in Michael's team. Michael called his approach the Heart of Success model. He couldn't have been more satisfied and excited. Now he only hoped it would just as quickly bring positive change to his business.

Sunday night he looked online to review the company's customer service reports and was alarmed to see the problems they were experiencing. Despite Sarah's best efforts to fix their customer service challenges, things looked like they were only getting worse. He couldn't wait to get to work on Monday and implement the Heart of Success model with his customer service team. If it worked with a basketball team so quickly, surely it would have an immediate impact at work—or so he thought.

Chapter 23

Failing

With sports teams you can tell if certain principles work. You know if a leader has the buy-in from their team. You know if a team is together and united. It's even clear during a 16-week football season. But with businesses and organizations, leadership and team-building principles often take a little longer to reveal measurable benefits and success. Michael, unfortunately, would learn this firsthand, as his business didn't rebound as quickly as his daughter's basketball team.

As soon as he arrived at work on Monday he called an all-employee meeting and shared the carpenter's three greatest success strategies along with the Heart of Success model with everyone. He talked about his recent health scare and his fear of losing his company and his life. Sarah also shared all they had been through and the challenges she faced. They were vulnerable and transparent about their obstacles as a family and the leaders of Social Connect, and yet they also expressed their passion, vision, and optimism for their future as a company.

The meeting rallied everyone around Sarah and Michael and their vision. They agreed on a short-term plan to acquire a few more customers to keep them afloat and improve customer service, and a long-term vision to grow and prosper.

Everyone knew what they needed to do and was excited about doing it. They made signs with paper hearts with the words *Love, Serve,* and *Care* and put them up around the office to remind everyone to go above and beyond for their clients.

Unfortunately, all this excitement didn't have an immediate impact. A week went by and they had yet to acquire a new customer. Then another week went by, and still no new customers. Michael was making one call after another with no success. He stayed positive and approached everyone and everything with love, and yet he had nothing to show for it. To make matters worse, their customer service wasn't getting any better despite their best efforts. Michael knew Social Connect was working to hire a few more people to handle the volume, but there were still other issues he couldn't quite solve. It was time to go see the carpenter.

Chapter 24

Success Takes Time

Michael found the carpenter at his favorite burrito shop after work. That's where his voicemail told people he would be. He was now working in a private home, like Michael and Sarah's, where it wouldn't be appropriate to have clients come see him, so he sat at the burrito shop for a few hours each day and waited for people to come visit him. He loved people watching and talking to strangers who needed to know they weren't alone in this world. He smiled, opened the door for people, and offered a word of encouragement to those he could tell needed it. Some thought he was too nice to be normal. Others thought he worked there. The burrito shop owners loved him because business always got busier when he was there. Everyone who came to see him bought something and became an instant fan of the place. But even the burrito shop's happy atmosphere could not convert Michael's misery. As he chomped on his burrito, he told the carpenter about his struggle to acquire new clients over the past few weeks.

"I thought Love, Serve, Care would work immediately, like it worked with the basketball team," he said.

The carpenter smiled. "It will work, but it takes time! These are not short-term success strategies. These are strategies for the long haul, strategies to build a masterpiece, not something you stick together with plywood. As they say, Rome wasn't built in a day, and neither will your business. Consider that Sam Walton did not open his second store until seven years after starting his company. Success requires perseverance. Starbucks did not reach store number five until 13 years into its history. John Wooden, my dear friend and one of the greatest coaches of all time, didn't win his first national title until his 16th season at UCLA. It was he who said, 'All great things take time.'

"Anything worthwhile takes time to build. We all want success now, but that's not how success works. After all, if we had immediate success, we wouldn't build the character we need to sustain true success. The struggle, adversity, triumphs, and victories are all part of the building process, and we must embrace all of it."

Chapter 25

The Gift of Failure

"But I'm failing," Michael said frantically. "I don't feel like I'm building anything. I feel like things are crumbling around me."

"We all fail," the carpenter said. "It's what we do after we fail that determines what we build in the long run. Some of the most successful people throughout history have experienced great failures, but they turned their great failures into great success. Most people don't know that Walt Disney was once fired from a newspaper for a lack of ideas, and his first cartoon production company went bankrupt. Everyone loves Lucy but Lucille Ball was told that she had no talent and should leave Murray Anderson's drama school. What would have happened if Dr. Seuss actually burned the manuscript of his first book, which he wanted to do after it was rejected by 27 publishers? And it's easy to forget that Steve Jobs was fired from Apple at 30 years old, and that Oprah Winfrey was fired as a news anchor and told she wasn't fit for television."

"I didn't know any of that," said Michael.

"Yes, it's true, and there are countless success stories just like theirs. I have worked in the homes of many successful people and have seen firsthand that everyone fails in life, but failure can be a gift if you don't give up and are willing to learn, improve, and grow because of it. You see, failure often serves as a defining moment, a crossroads on the journey of your life. It gives you a test designed to measure your courage, perseverance, commitment, and dedication. Are you a pretender who gives up after a little adversity or a contender who keeps getting up after getting knocked down?

"Failure provides you with a great opportunity to decide how much you really want something. Will you give up? Or will you dig deeper, commit more, work harder, learn, and get better? If you know that this is what you truly want, you will be willing to pay the price that success requires. You will be willing to fail again and again in order to succeed.

"Alternatively, sometimes failure causes you to take a different path that is better for you in the long run. My son failed in his first job out of college, but that led to him finding his dream job. Sometimes we have to lose a goal to find our destiny. Sometimes a failure helps us see that we really don't want that goal but we do want something else.

"Whatever path failure guides you toward, it is always meant to give you a big serving of humble pie that builds your character, gives you perspective, grows your faith, and makes you appreciate your success later on. If you didn't fail, you wouldn't become the kind of person who ultimately succeeds.

"I want to encourage you to see failure as a test, a teacher, a detour to a better outcome, and an event that builds a better you. Failure is not meant to be final and fatal. It is not meant to define you. It is meant to refine you to be all that you are meant to be. When you see failure as a blessing instead of a curse, you will turn the gift of failure into a stepping stone that leads to the gift of success."

"So what do I do now?" Michael asked.

The carpenter's answer wasn't what Michael expected, but it was exactly what he needed to hear.

Chapter 26

Unfinished Work

The carpenter ran his hand along the table. "I built this table," he said. "I built every table in here and also that bar railing over there. You know what they all have in common?"

"What?" asked Michael.

"They are all imperfect. They are all unfinished pieces of work. Yes, I call every one of my projects a masterpiece, but even a masterpiece has imperfections. Yes, I strive for perfection but I know it will never happen. There's no such thing as a perfect piece of wood, and there's no such thing as a perfect human being.

"Every struggle, every challenge, every failure is meant to help show us who we are in this moment and how far we have to go to become all we are meant to be. We see how imperfect we are and how much we fall short. We realize we are unfinished works of art, and our Creator who made us with love is not done with us yet. Once we realize this, we can allow ourselves to be shaped and molded to become all that God created us to be. Your plan may not be working perfectly, but there's a perfect plan working in you.

"So, you asked what you should do now. Learn from these recent failures and let them improve you as a leader, person, and builder. You're leading the company through these difficulties at this very moment for a reason. All of it is meant to help you grow and become a better leader and, most of all, a better person. Have a little faith, a lot of courage, and continue to get better. I believe in you."

Chapter 27

Courage

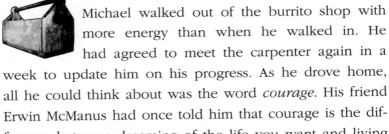

Michael walked out of the burrito shop with more energy than when he walked in. He had agreed to meet the carpenter again in a week to update him on his progress. As he drove home, all he could think about was the word *courage*. His friend Erwin McManus had once told him that courage is the difference between dreaming of the life you want and living the life of your dreams, but as Michael searched his heart, he didn't feel very courageous. He knew many stories of courageous people who had changed the world because of their courage. Yet knowing he needed courage to conquer his fears and having the courage to do so were entirely different matters.

He remembered a quote from Nelson Mandela that he had once heard and memorized: "Do not judge me by my successes, judge me by how many times I fell down and got back up again." Michael realized he had been listening to himself, thinking all that mattered was a successful outcome, but now he realized that what mattered most was that he bounced back from each failure and setback. The future wasn't certain. His plan may not work. He might fail. But he didn't have to focus on any of that. All he had to focus on was having the courage to get up and keep moving forward.

"Be courageous," he told himself as he clenched his fists. Fear had caused him to collapse once but would not again. Life's too short not to go after your dreams. "Life's too short to live in fear," he shouted as he looked in the rearview mirror. He didn't want to just be courageous for himself, but also for his family and everyone who believed in him. He knew that years from now his kids would be telling stories about him, and he wanted them to say that he was courageous, loving, and caring. He wanted them to know that he was willing to fail in order to succeed. He knew his life and the lessons his kids learned from him would be the greatest legacy he could leave them, and there was no way he was going to leave a legacy of fear and cowardice. Besides, he and Sarah didn't have a plan B. They had decided when they stepped out in faith to pursue their dream, they couldn't have a plan B, or it would be too easy to quit. There was no other option. Sure, their families criticized them, but they liked to say that everyone can be a critic but only the courageous create. Now he was at a crossroads. Let failure define him and let the critics have their day, or let his courage define him. There was no other way. He would be courageous and create the life of his dreams or fail trying.

He walked into the house and straight to his kids' bedrooms to write a message on their whiteboards. They might not fully understand what he was writing now, but over time he believed the message would serve them well.

No challenge can stop you if you have the courage to keep moving forward in the face of your greatest fears and biggest challenges. Be courageous.

Michael then walked to his office and with all the courage he could muster, he looked at the sales and customer service reports and began to devise a plan to succeed.

Chapter 28

A Glimmer of Hope

It happened like most great things do, when you least expect it. One of Michael's clients was talking to a friend about the great success his company was having because of Social Connect's software and it led to a sales call. It wasn't a huge sale, but it was enough to provide a glimmer of hope that Social Connect would be able to find enough new business to replace the loss of their biggest client.

Sarah and Michael were making progress but still had a long way to go in a short amount of time. They had a month to get a few more clients and avoid taking out a loan or taking on investors. Sarah told Michael that she felt like they were being carried, that somehow, some way it was going to work out. Michael was being courageous, but he was also being practical by thinking of the best funding options if they needed to take outside money to stay afloat.

In the meantime he got up every day, determined to create his masterpiece. He talked to himself instead of listening to himself, and even started to jog once again. *Love, Serve,* and *Care* were becoming more than words at his company. They were serving as a foundation for everything Social Connect did. Michael and Sarah noticed, their employees noticed, and they just hoped their clients would notice before it was too late.

The following week more referrals came in, but they didn't close any more new business. Michael knew how much effort they were putting into their sales and service, and he expected more. They hired more customer service people and even invested in the continuous improvement of their software, but one new client did not provide enough revenue to offset the additional costs. Michael was trying to be courageous, but he was frustrated. In a fit of anger he punched his desk so hard that he broke it. It was a private moment of frustration, and while he had done a great job controlling his emotions at basketball practice and home, he was still upset with himself for letting his anger get the best of him. He knew what the carpenter had said was true; Michael was a work in progress. When they saw each other later that day, Michael hoped J. would have some answers for him, as well as some time to fix his desk.

As Michael walked into the burrito shop, a woman was walking out, waving to the carpenter and saying, "Thank you so much for saving my life. I'll call you about the shed."

"What happened?" Michael asked as he sat down at the carpenter's table.

"Oh, nothing. She was just choking on a piece of steak and I gave her the Heimlich maneuver."

"Do you just walk around the city like a superhero looking for opportunities to save people?" Michael asked, laughing out loud. "Now I know your real secret for getting so much business."

J. laughed. "It happens to me all the time. I'm always out and about somewhere. I like to meet people and I make myself available. When you are available, opportunities to be of service present themselves. Somehow there's always someone who needs to be saved, and I always seem to be in the right place at the right time to help out."

"Just like when I went down?"

"Yes, and like with you, it often leads to a relationship where we wind up building something great together. I guess it happens so often I don't think it's that strange anymore."

"Oh, it's very strange, but I sure am glad you were strangely there for me," Michael said while laughing. He didn't know what it was but just being around the carpenter made him feel better and happier. "And speaking of being there for me, I need to ask you a favor before I ask for your guidance. My desk broke today and I was wondering if you had time to fix it tomorrow."

"Well it just so happens that I finished a job today and my next client had an emergency, so I have an opening this week. But I don't want to just fix your desk; I want to build you a special J. Emmanuel desk. I can write down what kind of wood you need to get and, if you have it there when I arrive, I can get started immediately. Would that work?" he asked.

"That would be fantastic," Michael said as he looked around and realized a bunch of people were waiting to talk to and hire the carpenter.

J. noticed the people as well, but he wanted to give Michael his full attention, knowing he needed some guidance. "What else did you need help with?" he asked.

Michael looked at the line of people, which was growing by the minute. "It's okay. It can wait. You have a bunch of people waiting to talk to you, and we can just talk tomorrow. Do you need a ride? My office is a lot farther than my house," he said as he wrote his business address on a card.

"No, it's fine. I'll take a bus halfway and walk the rest. Who knows; maybe I'll save someone else tomorrow on my way," he said, laughing out loud while patting Michael on the back.

Chapter 29

Be the Mission

As the carpenter built a new desk for Michael, they talked about the latest challenges at Social Connect. Michael shared all they had been doing to put Love, Serve, Care into action, and the frustrating results of acquiring only one new customer.

"I see it differently," said the carpenter. "I believe you should be thankful that you got a new customer. The more you are thankful, the more you will have things to be thankful for. The more you and your company appreciate each new client, the more you will become a magnet for new clients. This appears to be a wonderful growth opportunity for you and your company," he said with a warm smile.

Michael nodded, knowing the carpenter was right. He had been focused on what Social Connect lacked instead of what it had. He had been looking through the lens of pessimism instead of opportunity.

"You also have to remember what I told you the other day," J. said. "Success takes time. Clients won't recognize all that you are doing to love, serve, and care right away. The outside world won't immediately see what you are doing on the inside. You won't always be recognized. That's okay. Just keep doing the work. Keep loving, serving, and caring. Keep making a difference. Over time people will notice, word will spread, and the truth will shine through."

The carpenter picked up a piece of wood that would become one of the desk's legs. "Everyone wants the quick-fix solution. They want convenient, immediate success. They don't want to get messy. But there's nothing convenient about loving everyone we are meant to love. There's nothing easy about serving others when your own life is challenging and you want someone to serve you. Sometimes it's hard to care when you don't feel like caring."

"It's not easy at all. Love, Serve, Care sounds so simple, but it takes a lot to truly live it," Michael said as he looked at the Heart of Success model on his wall. "It's easy to have a great mission statement, but it's pointless unless your people are on a mission."

"That is a powerful truth," the carpenter said. "That's why you can't just talk about the mission; you have to *be* the mission. Everyone on your team and in your business must live it, breathe it, and share it.

"You need to dig down and love deeper, serve greater, and care more. The love of what you are building has to be greater than the challenges you face. Serve greater! Become a mighty servant who serves in small ways, big ways, and sideways. Serve everyone as if they are the only person on the planet. And care more. Care so much that you care enough for everyone." The carpenter could tell Michael was a little overwhelmed. Michael was already doing all that the carpenter asked but now he was asking even more of him. But that's what great coaches do. They push you beyond your limits and past your comfort zone. Getting Michael to do more was the only way to build something great.

"Do you know what drives us to love deeper, serve greater, and care more?" J. asked.

"I have to *be* the mission?" asked Michael.

"Yes," J. answered, "but there's something before the mission. The key is finding the purpose that inspires you to be the mission. Let's face it, you won't always feel very optimistic. There will be days you don't want to get out of bed. You will have moments when the last thing you want to do is to love, serve, and care. It is during these times that you need to remember your purpose. When you know your why, you will know the way and you'll find a way. Your purpose will inspire you to love those who are hard to love, serve when you don't feel like serving, and care more when you don't feel very caring."

"So how do I put this into practice?" asked Michael. "And how do I help my team love deeper, serve greater, and care more?"

The carpenter picked up another piece of wood to measure it. "You and your team complete this sentence: 'I love, serve, and care because_____.' When you can complete this sentence you will become a powerful success builder. And if you do what I tell you next, you will become one of the greatest success builders on the planet."

Chapter 30

All for One

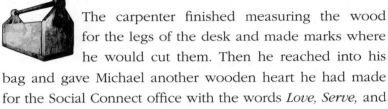
The carpenter finished measuring the wood for the legs of the desk and made marks where he would cut them. Then he reached into his bag and gave Michael another wooden heart he had made for the Social Connect office with the words *Love, Serve,* and *Care* already carved into it. Then he said, "Once you know why you love, serve, and care, then you share it all with one person at a time. You gather all your love, all your desire to serve, all your care, and you give it to one person, one moment, one interaction at a time.

"You see, it's easy to get overwhelmed when you think about having to implement Love, Serve, Care with all your team members and all your customers and all the people you interact with. It's easy to put these systems and programs in place yet manage to not love, serve, and care for the people who are right in front of you. You get so overwhelmed with the prospect of having to do this for everyone that you wind up doing it for no one. You start to believe you can't make a difference, so you don't. But the truth is you *can* make a difference.

"It's like the two friends walking on the beach who come across a bunch of starfish stranded on the shore. One person starts picking up starfish and throwing them back into the ocean. The other friend asks, 'Why are you doing that? There are so many starfish stranded on the beach, you can't possibly help them all.' The first friend then picks another starfish up and throws it back in the ocean, and says, 'I made a difference for that one.'

"In this spirit, the key to becoming a powerful success builder is to make a difference to one person, one moment at a time. You do it each day, with each person, in each moment, as part of each interaction, and over time you powerfully impact a lot of people. Always remember that a big mission starts with a small group of people. If you want to impact millions of people, you have to start with one. If you want to impact billions, start with twelve, one person at a time."

Michael nodded as he thought about his daughter's youth basketball team and realized the power of what the carpenter was saying. With the 12 girls on his team, he focused on one interaction at a time and saw a powerful impact. He also saw this play out at the new hair salon Sarah had just found. When Michael was there waiting for his daughter to get her hair cut, he met the owner, Frank, and asked him why his place was so busy. Frank said he had a simple secret to success. When a young girl sits in his chair, he treats her like he would his daughter. When a woman about his age sits in his chair, he treats her like he would his wife. When an older woman sits in his chair, he treats her like he would his mother. Frank treats his customers like family, and his business just grows and grows.

Yet, Michael wasn't doing this with his team at work, and they weren't doing it with customer service. They were too focused on their big problems to see such a small, simple, powerful solution. It wasn't about loving, serving, and caring for *everyone* all at once. It was about loving, serving, and caring for *one person at a time*. Michael knew what he needed to do immediately, but before he left to go meet with Sarah and his team, the carpenter had one final piece of advice for him. "What I am about to tell you may seem counterintuitive because we've been talking about strategies to build your business, but the key to loving, serving, and caring for one person at a time is this: *Don't focus on building your business. Focus on using your business to Love, Serve, Care, and build others up. If you do this, your business will build and multiply exponentially.*"

"It is counterintuitive, but I get it," said Michael. It made perfect sense to him. His experience as a coach had taught him that if you want to win a basketball game, you shouldn't focus on winning. You should focus on the process it takes to win. His favorite coaching quote was: *Don't focus on winning a championship, focus on becoming a champion*. He knew that champions made plays that won championships.

He also focused on the process as a parent. He often told his children not to worry about grades but to be their best every day and they would do great. He and Sarah taught them the right habits and knew their habits would lead to great results.

Yet at work he didn't make the process the focus, and knew his team needed to hear what their focus really should be. It wasn't about building the business. Their job was to Love, Serve, Care, and build others up. If they did this each moment in each interaction, Social Connect would grow. It was so simple Michael wanted to kick himself for forgetting what he knew to be true. Unfortunately, he thought it might be too late since it would take time for this approach to translate into more business, and it would take a miracle for them to acquire a few more clients before their funding ran out. But there was no other option. He couldn't wait a minute longer. He had to share the carpenter's advice immediately.

"I'll see you in a little bit. I'm going to build others up," Michael said before thanking J. for his advice and walking out the door to meet with his team and company.

Chapter 31

Progress

The next week was the best ever in the history of the company. Not in terms of financial success because they still didn't acquire more clients, but Michael could feel the shift happen as everyone focused on Love, Serve, Care with each other, each customer, and each sales call. Sarah and Michael decided they would no longer measure success by how much money they made, but rather by the people who were impacted by their love, service, and caring—and of course their software. Ironically, they sold technology that connected the digital and physical worlds, but their biggest priority was to create human connections. If they focused on the process they would love what the process produced.

With their new approach, their customer service improved dramatically. Their customer service scores were at an all-time high and even though their employees were caring more and giving more to each interaction, they were also more energized than ever. Sarah told Michael that caring more doesn't make you tired. It energizes you and others. She also said that hard work doesn't make you tired. A bad attitude and belief that you aren't making a difference is what makes you tired. Michael was glad he had married a woman who was a lot smarter than he was.

Together they championed their one-person-at-a-time approach to everyone in the company and also decided to model it for each other. They talked about the fact that if you don't have strong leadership at the top, the organization will crumble at the bottom. They knew the success of their family and business started with them and their relationship. Through all the struggles and challenges they needed to be a unified, strong team.

"Whatever happens, we'll get through this and we'll be stronger than ever," she said.

"I know," he said, trying to be optimistic. He was trying not to think about the future too much. He was doing his best to heed the carpenter's advice and focus on one day at a time, one person at a time. He still had a few weeks left to save his business and knew it would be up to him to get a few more clients. In the past, this realization caused him to collapse, but ever since the carpenter had saved him, he became stronger, more focused, and better prepared to take on the challenges he was facing. Michael said the phrases the carpenter had taught him, even when he didn't feel like saying them. When he woke up feeling negative in the morning he made a decision to be optimistic and attack each day with courage. When he felt discouraged during the day, he read the positive pledge and focused on his purpose. He didn't want to just build a company; he wanted to change the world.

And when fear and self-doubt enveloped him and he wanted to give up, Michael made a decision to keep moving forward, believing that somehow, some way it would all work out. He acted like the outcome depended on him, and he prayed like it depended on God. His family and his family's future were in jeopardy, and he would give everything he had to provide for them.

Chapter 32

Everything Is Spiritual

At the end of the week, the carpenter was putting his final touches on the new desk when Michael walked into his office. The desk was magnificent. He was speechless as he marveled at the carpenter's talent, and wondered how someone could create such beauty with pieces of wood. After a long pause he asked in a quiet voice, "How do you do what you do?"

The carpenter smiled. "It's because I know who I am."

"Of course you do. You are J. Emmanuel, a craftsman masquerading as a carpenter," Michael said with a big smile.

"It's more than that," said the carpenter. "I know that I'm not a human being having a spiritual experience. I'm a spiritual being having a human experience. While I have a body, it is my soul and spirit that power me. Artists create from the depths of their souls. An artist is moved by the spirit. I know who I am, and I know the power that moves me to create."

Then he paused and rubbed his hand along the smooth surface of the desk. "You know we can all create with this power, but too many people have forgotten who they truly are. Two thousand years ago there was no separation between someone's work life and spiritual life. Now we separate them and wonder why people are so miserable. Work is meant to be a spiritual experience, not a daily chore and a grind. All work is sacred. Everything is spiritual. When you bring your spirit to work you will become a powerful builder of success."

Then with a big smile on his face the carpenter gestured for Michael to come sit in his chair at his new desk. The moment Michael sat down he could feel there was something different about the desk, and he knew everything the carpenter was saying was true. "Wow," was all he could say.

"Yes," J. continued. "When you realize everything is spiritual, you don't just build great things, you build with great power. Whether it's a team, a business, a school, or software, your spirit and soul should define all that you build. Your work should be a reflection of the very best within you. You are meant to create and build from the depths of your soul. When you build in this way, it will be one of the most powerful, amazing experiences you'll ever have.

"People will ask you how you did it, and it will be hard to explain. But your work and effort won't need an explanation. Like this desk, your spirit and soul will be on display for the entire world to see, and they'll know there's something different about you. They'll know there's something more powerful moving in you. Most will think that you are special, and there's no way they can create like you can. Some will realize this gift is meant for everyone and they can do it too. They'll ask you how it's done and you'll tell them because success is meant to be shared, and if they listen and follow your advice, together you'll build great things and change the world."

The carpenter then walked toward Michael and gave him a hug good-bye. "You are ready, my friend, to build even greater things. I have shared with you all that I know and I'm excited for you and your future. Please come see me and let me know how the next few weeks go. I'm expecting to hear great things."

"I will," said Michael, who in that moment didn't share the carpenter's optimism. As he thought about what he still had to do to save his company, he felt more fearful and less spiritual than ever.

Chapter 33

Creating the Impossible

Michael wanted to build the kind of business where people would ask him how he did it, and every day as he sat at his desk he was reminded of the lessons the carpenter had taught him. He truly hoped J. was right about everything being spiritual, especially since he kept praying for a miracle. With two weeks to go, he and Sarah needed something miraculous to happen or else their business and dream would be dead.

He thought they would easily be able to raise money from investors, but everyone he met with balked because Social Connect had already lost their biggest client. It raised too many red flags, and Social Connect was considered a very risky proposition. Investors figured that when the company went bankrupt its intellectual property could be bought for pennies on the dollar, so why take the risk now?

Michael knew that as soon as their biggest client's contract ended, Social Connect would run out of money very quickly without additional funding. Even if they secured several new clients in the next two weeks they wouldn't see the revenue right away, and without support from investors, he had to find other funding to keep them afloat until new client revenue came in. That is, if he was even able to acquire new clients.

He remembered reading about Fred Smith, the founder of FedEx, who, in the early days of the company, was faced with a similar situation. He didn't even have enough money to make payroll, pay for their jet fuel, and keep the company afloat. Legend has it that he took whatever money was in the account, went to Las Vegas, and won enough at the blackjack table to keep FedEx going until they secured additional funding. Michael wasn't about to go to Las Vegas, but he was on his way to the bank to bet his family's future and secure a second mortgage on their home. If they lost their business, they would lose their home too. Michael knew it wasn't the smartest thing, but it was the only thing he could do to secure funding and keep his company afloat a little bit longer while he tried to create the impossible.

On his way back from the bank, he decided if they lost it all they would start over. He agreed with the carpenter and believed that the spiritual creates the physical, and ideas and principles are what build lasting success. He felt equipped with the right tools, principles, and strategies to build something else if Social Connect should crumble. They could take his business and his home, but no one could take what he had learned from the carpenter. No one could destroy his spirit. No one could stop him from changing the world. It wouldn't be easy, and for a while he and his family would lose all of the comforts they now enjoyed. But he was willing to endure the struggle and pain in order to live his purpose and follow his dream.

The fear he felt turned into faith, and his faith turned into trust that no matter what happened, they would be okay. He trusted in a bigger plan for his life and let go of the outcome. In what should have been the most fearful time of his life, he actually became the most peaceful and spiritual. He poured his heart and soul into every aspect of his business, and worked harder than he ever had, but didn't feel stressed or tired.

A week later, with no new clients to celebrate, all seemed hopeless. Several sales leads had dried up and only a few referrals had come in. The prospect of securing several new clients appeared bleak to everyone. The business was about to crumble. Michael calmly accepted their fate and was preparing to lose everything and start over.

But when all seems hopeless, that's when miracles happen. That's when the physical gives way to the spiritual, and the impossible becomes possible. That's when things you can't explain happen and change your life forever. That's when Michael and Sarah got a random call from a reporter from the local business journal.

She said she wanted to do a story about couples building a business together. She came to interview them for an article profiling 10 power couples in tech city. Michael and Sarah didn't think much about it. A few days later the article ran, and their office phones wouldn't stop ringing. The story was supposed to include a brief mention about them, but the reporter decided to make it a feature on them and their company. As part of the story the reporter interviewed several clients who sang Social Connect's praises, gushing about their revolutionary software and customer-centric approach.

Even more miraculous, the reporter didn't interview the client who was leaving them because of their past mistakes.

That week they received more inbound sales leads and referrals than they did in the previous three months combined. It was as if they were living the carpenter's words. Success takes time. It doesn't happen overnight. People don't always recognize you right away. But with this article, the truth shined through and their soul and spirit were on display for the world to see. At a time when it seemed all was lost, they found not just two more clients, but five more clients.

A few months later, Michael and Sarah stood at the bank together crying and hugging. As their last dime was leaving their account to pay expenses, together they deposited checks from their new clients. The timing couldn't have been more perfect.

Chapter 34

Build

With their Love, Serve, Care model, Sarah, Michael, and Social Connect were able to successfully serve their five new clients, hire more employees, receive more referrals, and continue to improve their software. They received a lot of attention for their software, but became even more known for their *Heart of Success* business model. Each year they won "the best place to work award" but they never took it for granted. Instead they stayed humble and hungry, and looked for ways to love deeper, serve greater, and care more. Michael told everyone that when you focus on one person, one moment at a time, and build your business with the principles based on *The Way*, you can't help but grow. Michael wrote down everything the carpenter had told him, and created a success-builder manual that described the core principles and strategies of the company.

True to the carpenter's words, their business continued to build. Five new clients turned into 20 new clients, which turned into 100 new clients. Social Connect grew so fast that they had to move into a bigger office building, and guess who did all the carpentry work for it? Michael finally admitted to himself that the carpenter was the best marketer in the world.

Michael learned that when you help others build their business, your business will grow as well. When you help others improve their lives, your life will improve. When you help a team member be better, you'll get better.

Michael thought about this every day as he sat at his J. Emmanuel desk. It was a reminder to use his work and life to love, serve, and care, and build others up. He promised himself no matter how big his business grew and how successful he became, he would always remember to impact one person at a time the way the carpenter had taken the time to help him.

Chapter 35

Success Is Meant to Be Shared

A few years later, Michael jogged to see the carpenter at his latest job site. It had become his morning ritual to run to wherever J. was working in the city. They would spend a little time together to talk and prepare for the day ahead. The carpenter always shared encouraging advice that Michael needed to hear and, in turn, Michael would share it with others.

When Michael arrived the carpenter said, "Wow, you are here even earlier than yesterday."

"I left the same time as yesterday but I'm getting faster," said Michael. "My new motto is older, stronger, faster, and better."

"That's what I call talking to yourself," the carpenter said, laughing.

"I learned from the best."

"So what are we building this week?" asked the carpenter.

"I'm helping a school principal build her school's culture. Then, I'm meeting with a hospital's leadership team and sharing your model with them. Then, I'm meeting with a friend of a friend who asked me to share Love, Serve, Care with all the coaches at his college."

"A busy week," the carpenter said proudly. Michael may not have been handy, but he had a gift for building up people and helping leaders build their teams and J. was proud of him and all he was doing to help others.

"It keeps getting busier," Michael said. "And don't forget we start building a new set of homes for the people our foundation selected. We start Saturday morning."

"I'll be there. You know I never miss an opportunity to build and change a life," the carpenter said as he patted Michael on the back. The carpenter had always told Michael, *"You will build even greater things than I,"* and over time Michael began to believe him. The carpenter had also told him to keep dreaming of the things he wanted to build, and imagine the future as it should be. Then take actions to create it. He said that too many people stop dreaming and then they stop living. And in one of the most powerful lessons of all he said, *"You aren't a true success unless you are helping others be successful. Success is meant to be shared."*

As Michael jogged home he thought about all that he wanted to do to help others be successful, and all that he and the carpenter had built together. They started out building an entertainment center. Then they built a desk, and then his business. Now they were building so much more. Michael and Sarah dreamed of building homes for people who couldn't afford one, and they did. They started with one and, as their business, profits, and influence in their city grew, they built more and more. Then they dreamed of building a school in Africa, and they did that as well with the support of friends and business partners. When his children asked why they were doing all this, Michael and Sarah taught them that the success you create now is temporary, but the legacy you leave is eternal. They believed the goal in life was not to accumulate things, but to give your life away. And the best way to give your life away was to help others build things that make a difference.

Michael and Sarah contributed large sums of money to their foundation, and their foundation also sold wooden hearts, handcrafted by the carpenter, with the words *Love, Serve,* and *Care* carved into the surface. Their goal was to spread Love, Serve, Care everywhere.

The more money they raised, the more they gave away. The more they helped others be successful, the more they built for others, the more their own business grew. They learned the powerful law of generosity. The more you give, the more you will receive to give away. And so, every year they made more and gave more away.

Michael ran faster down the street as he thought about new dreams and new projects he wanted to build. As he approached a main intersection, he saw a car swerve and try to avoid a young man on his bicycle. It was early, the streets were quiet, and unfortunately the driver didn't maneuver fast enough. The car clipped the back wheel, causing the bike and the man to fall and hit the pavement. Michael sprinted to the young man, called 911, and used his towel to stop the man's head from bleeding. The young man, who looked like he was in his twenties, was conscious but in pain. He had a bunch of scrapes and cuts on his arms and legs. When the ambulance arrived, the EMTs told Michael the man's injuries were mostly on the surface; there were possibly a few broken ribs, but nothing life threatening.

"He's very lucky," Michael said as he thought about the day he collapsed years ago, the day his life changed forever. He handed the ambulance driver his card to give to the young man. It wasn't a fancy card. Michael had learned the greatest marketing strategy of all could not fit on a card, and it didn't involve telling someone how great you were. The greatest marketing strategy of all was doing something great for someone else.

The young man and his family looked at the card in the hospital. It was a simple white card with black ink that said "Builder" and had Michael's phone number on it.

The End!

Tools for Success

Visit www.Carpenter11.com to:

- Print posters with memorable quotes from the book.
- Share the carpenter's strategies with your organization and team.
- Watch videos.
- Share the Heart of Success model with others.
- Invite your team to Love, Serve, Care.
- Order *The Carpenter* action plans to implement the strategies in the book.
- Order wooden shaped hearts for you and your organization. All proceeds go to charity.

Bring the Greatest Success Principles to Your Team and Organization

If you are interested in implementing the Heart of Success model with your leaders, organization, and/or team, contact the Jon Gordon Companies at:

Phone: (904) 285-6842

E-mail: info@jongordon.com

Online: JonGordon.com

Twitter: @jongordon11

Facebook: Facebook.com/JonGordonpage

Instagram: JonGordon11

Sign up for Jon Gordon's weekly e-newsletter at JonGordon.com

To purchase bulk copies of *The Carpenter* at a discount for large groups or your organization, please contact your favorite bookseller or Wiley's Special Sales group at specialsales@wiley.com or (800) 762-2974.

Other Books by Jon Gordon

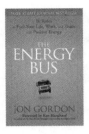

The Energy Bus
A man whose life and career are in shambles learns from a unique bus driver and set of passengers how to overcome adversity. Enjoy an enlightening ride of positive energy that is improving the way leaders lead, employees work, and teams function.
www.TheEnergyBus.com

The No Complaining Rule
Follow a VP of Human Resources who must save herself and her company from ruin, and discover proven principles and an actionable plan to win the battle against individual and organizational negativity.
www.NoComplainingRule.com

Training Camp
This inspirational story about a small guy with a big heart, and a special coach who guides him on a quest for excellence, reveals the eleven winning habits that separate the best individuals and teams from the rest.
www.TrainingCamp11.com

The Shark and the Goldfish
Delightfully illustrated, this quick read is packed with tips and strategies on how to respond to challenges beyond your control in order to thrive during waves of change.
www.SharkandGoldfish.com

Soup
The newly appointed CEO of a popular soup company is brought in to reinvigorate the brand and bring success back to a company that has fallen on hard times. Through her journey, discover the key ingredients to unite, engage, and inspire teams to create a culture of greatness.
www.Soup11.com

The Seed
Go on a quest for the meaning and passion behind work with Josh, an up-and-comer at his company who is disenchanted with his job. Through Josh's cross-country journey, you'll find surprising new sources of wisdom and inspiration in your own business and life.
www.Seed11.com

One Word
One Word is a simple concept that delivers powerful life change! This quick read will inspire you to simplify your life and work by focusing on just one word for this year. *One Word* creates clarity, power, passion, and life-change. When you find your word, live it, and share it, your life will become more rewarding and exciting than ever.
www.getoneword.com

The Positive Dog
We all have two dogs inside of us. One dog is positive, happy, optimistic, and hopeful. The other dog is negative, mad, pessimistic, and fearful. These two dogs often fight inside us, but guess who wins? The one you feed the most. *The Positive Dog* is an inspiring story that not only reveals the strategies and benefits of being positive, but also an essential truth: being positive doesn't just make you better; it makes everyone around you better.
www.feedthepositivedog.com

The Hard Hat
A true story about Cornell lacrosse player George Boiardi, *The Hard Hat* is an unforgettable book about a selfless, loyal, joyful, hard-working, competitive, and compassionate leader and teammate, the impact he had on his team and program, and the lessons we can learn from him. This inspirational story will teach you how to build a great team and be the best teammate you can be.

www.hardhat21.com

You Win in the Locker Room First
Based on the extraordinary experiences of NFL Coach Mike Smith and leadership expert Jon Gordon, *You Win in the Locker Room First* offers a rare, behind-the-scenes look at one of the most pressure-packed leadership jobs on the planet, and what leaders can learn from these experiences in order to build their own winning teams.

www.wininthelockerroom.com

Life Word
Life Word reveals a simple, powerful tool to help you identify the word that will inspire you to live your best life while leaving your greatest legacy. In the process, you'll discover your *why*, which will help show you how to live with a renewed sense of power, purpose, and passion.

www.getoneword.com/lifeword

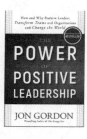

The Power of Positive Leadership

The Power of Positive Leadership is your personal coach for becoming the leader your people deserve. Jon Gordon gathers insights from his bestselling fables to bring you the definitive guide to positive leadership. Difficult times call for leaders who are up for the challenge. Results are the byproduct of your culture, teamwork, vision, talent, innovation, execution, and commitment. This book shows you how to bring it all together to become a powerfully positive leader.

www.powerofpositiveleadership.com

The Energy Bus Field Guide

The Energy Bus Field Guide is your roadmap to fueling your life, work, and team with positive energy. The international bestseller, *The Energy Bus*, has helped millions of people from around the world shift to a more positive outlook. This guide is a practical companion to help you *live and share* the ten principles from *The Energy Bus* every day, with real, actionable steps you can immediately put into practice in your life, work, team, and organization.

The Power of a Positive Team

In *The Power of a Positive Team*, Jon Gordon draws upon his unique team building experience, as well as conversations with some of the greatest teams in history, to provide an essential framework of proven practices to empower teams to work together more effectively and achieve superior results.

www.PowerOfAPositiveTeam.com

The Coffee Bean
From bestselling author Jon Gordon and rising star Damon West comes *The Coffee Bean:* an illustrated fable that teaches readers how to transform their environment, overcome challenges, and create positive change.

The Energy Bus for Kids
The illustrated children's adaptation of the bestselling book, *The Energy Bus*, tells the story of George, who, with the help of his school bus driver, Joy, learns that if he believes in himself, he'll find the strength to overcome any challenge. His journey teaches kids how to overcome negativity, bullies, and everyday challenges to be their best.
    www.EnergyBusKids.com

Thank You and Good Night
Thank You and Good Night is a beautifully illustrated book that shares the heart of gratitude. Jon Gordon takes a little boy and girl on a fun-filled journey from one perfect moonlit night to the next. During their adventurous days and nights, the children explore the people, places, and things they are thankful for.

The Hard Hat for Kids
The Hard Hat for Kids is an illustrated guide to teamwork. Adapted from the bestseller *The Hard Hat*, this uplifting story presents practical insights and life-changing lessons that are immediately applicable to everyday situations, giving kids—and adults—a new outlook on cooperation, friendship, and the selfless nature of true teamwork.
    www.HardHatforKids.com